Available soon:

For more information visit our web site

www.oup.co.uk/general/vsi/

Eric H. Cline

THE TROJAN WAR

A Very Short Introduction

OXFORD
UNIVERSITY PRESS

OXFORD
UNIVERSITY PRESS

Oxford University Press is a department of the University of Oxford.
It furthers the University's objective of excellence in research,
scholarship, and education by publishing worldwide.

Oxford   New York
Auckland   Cape Town   Dar es Salaam   Hong Kong   Karachi
Kuala Lumpur   Madrid   Melbourne   Mexico City   Nairobi
New Delhi   Shanghai   Taipei   Toronto

With offices in
Argentina   Austria   Brazil   Chile   Czech Republic   France   Greece
Guatemala   Hungary   Italy   Japan   Poland   Portugal   Singapore
South Korea   Switzerland   Thailand   Turkey   Ukraine   Vietnam

Oxford is a registered trademark of Oxford University Press
in the UK and certain other countries.

Published in the United States of America by
Oxford University Press
198 Madison Avenue, New York, NY 10016

© Eric H. Cline 2013

All rights reserved. No part of this publication may be reproduced,
stored in a retrieval system, or transmitted, in any form or by any means,
without the prior permission in writing of Oxford University Press, or
as expressly permitted by law, by license, or under terms agreed with the
appropriate reproduction rights organization. Inquiries concerning
reproduction outside the scope of the above should be sent to the Rights
Department, Oxford University Press, at the address above.

You must not circulate this work in any other form, and you must
impose the same condition on any acquirer.

Library of Congress Cataloging-in-Publication Data
Cline, Eric H.
The Trojan War : a very short introduction / Eric H. Cline.
p.   cm.—(Very short introductions)
Includes bibliographical references and index.
ISBN 978-0-19-976027-5 (alk. paper)
1. Troy (Extinct city) 2. Trojan War. 3. Turkey—Antiquities.
4. Excavations (Archaeology)—Turkey—Troy (Extinct city)
5. Greece—Civilization—To 146 B.C. I. Title.
DF221.T8C54   2013
939'.21—dc23   2012036331

1 3 5 7 9 8 6 4 2

Printed in Great Britain
by Ashford Colour Press Ltd., Gosport, Hants.
on acid-free paper

*Dedicated to the memory of my mother,
for introducing me to the wonders of the Trojan War
when I was seven years old.*

Contents

List of illustrations

Acknowledgments

This book is a very short introduction to the Trojan War and the discovery and excavation of Troy/Hisarlik, written along the lines of the seminar course that I have taught several times at George Washington University. I have written previously about the Trojan War, including various scholarly articles, a book for young adults co-authored with Jill Rubalcaba (*Digging for Troy: From Homer to Hisarlik*; Charlesbridge, 2010), and a course guide that accompanied my audio lectures (*Archaeology and the Iliad: The Trojan War in Homer and History*; The Modern Scholar/Recorded Books, 2006). The present text represents an update in every instance, including recent re-examinations and interpretations of this much-studied subject.

I would like to thank my editor, Nancy Toff, for her marvelous efforts, as usual, and her assistant, Sonia Tycko; my wife, Diane Harris Cline; my father, Martin J. Cline; and two anonymous readers for OUP, for all reading through the entire manuscript and making editorial changes and suggestions. I would also like to thank Ed White at The Modern Scholar/Recorded Books for permission to use and rework the material originally published in conjunction with my audio course; Eric Shanower, Christoph Haußner, Trevor Bryce, Carol Hershenson and the Classics Department at the University of Cincinnati, and Peter Jablonka and the Troia Project at the University of Tübingen for illustrations; Carol Bell, John Bennet, Joshua W. Cannon, Erwin F. Cook, Oliver Dickinson, Peter Jablonka, Susan Sherratt, Rik A. Vaessen, and Erik van Dongen for bibliographic references and pdfs of articles; my students at GWU for their patience as I tried out new material on them over the course of the past several years; and, as always, my family for their usual forbearance.

The Trojan War

1. The Late Bronze Age Aegean and Western Anatolia, ca. 1250 BCE, including the major sites on mainland Greece, Crete, the Cycladic Islands, and the western coast of Turkey (Anatolia).

Introduction

Was there a conflict sometime back in antiquity that gave rise
to the legend of the Trojan War? Did the battles of that war take
place near the site that we now call Troy? The ancient Greeks
and Romans certainly thought that such a war had taken place,
and they thought they knew the site of its battles, in northwest
Anatolia (modern Turkey). Later, they built their own cities,
Hellenistic Ilion and Roman Ilium, respectively, at the same
location. It is said that Alexander the Great even slept with a
copy of the *Iliad* annotated by Aristotle under his pillow and
visited the presumed site of Troy during his Asian campaign in
334 BCE.

The Greeks and Romans believed that the Trojan War was both
a real event and a pivotal point in world history; Herodotus and
Thucydides discussed the Trojan War briefly in the opening pages
of their respective books, written during the fifth century BCE.
However, none of the later Greco-Roman scholars and authors
was quite certain when it had actually happened. Estimates for the
date of the war, including those by Herodotus, ranged from 1334
BCE to 1135 BCE, but those estimates were usually based on little
substantive evidence; dates were put forth as "a thousand years
before Alexander the Great's visit" or "eight hundred years before
the time of Herodotus." Eventually, the third-century BCE Greek
geographer Eratosthenes's estimated date of 1184 BCE ("407 years

before the first Olympiad") became the most favored, although it too was based mostly on guesswork.

Classical scholars during the Middle Ages and into the early modern era were more dubious and frequently minimized the importance of the Trojan War, or even dismissed it entirely as a piece of fiction. Only when Heinrich Schliemann, the so-called father of Mycenaean archaeology, claimed to have again located the site of Troy in the 1870s was attention seriously paid to the possibility that the story may have had a basis in historical reality, with interest focused on his newly excavated remains at the site of Hisarlik (Turkish *Hisarlık*, "Place of Fortresses"). Since then, scholarly discussion has continued unabated, with academic debate focused on several areas, including the literary evidence and the archaeological data for the existence of—and specific details concerning—Homer, Bronze Age Greece, Troy, and the Trojan War itself (see fig. 2).

The tale of the war, as related by Homer in the eighth century BCE, and by other Greek poets and playwrights in the centuries following, contains themes that have resonated down through the ages. The basic story, a timeless epic of love and war, rivalry and greed, heroes and cowards, is easily told. It revolves around a few central characters and a host of supporting actors. Those immediately central to the story include, on the one side, Helen, the wife of the Mycenaean Greek king of Sparta, Menelaus; Menelaus's brother Agamemnon, king of Mycenae; Achilles, a Mycenaean warrior from Thessaly who is almost without equal in battle; and Odysseus, the Mycenaean king of Ithaca. On the other side are, among others, Paris, the son of King Priam of Troy; Priam himself; and Hector, an older son of Priam.

The story of the Trojan War has fascinated humans for centuries and has given rise to countless scholarly articles and books, extensive archaeological excavations, epic movies, television documentaries, stage plays, art and sculpture, souvenirs and

2. After retiring from a successful business career, the wealthy Heinrich Schliemann devoted the rest of his life to finding and excavating Troy.

collectibles. In the United States there are thirty-three states with cities or towns named Troy and ten four-year colleges and universities, besides the University of Southern California, whose sports teams are called the Trojans. Particularly captivating is the account of the Trojan Horse, the daring plan that brought the Trojan War to an end and that has also entered modern parlance by giving rise to the saying "Beware of Greeks bearing gifts" and serving as a metaphor for hackers intent on wreaking havoc by inserting a "Trojan horse" into computer systems.

But, is Homer's story convincing? Certainly the heroes, from Achilles to Hector, are portrayed so credibly that it is easy to believe the story. But is it truly an account based on real events, and were the main characters actually real people? Would the ancient world's equivalent of the entire nation of Greece really have gone to war over a single woman, however beautiful, and for ten long years at that? Could Agamemnon really have been a king of kings able to muster so many men for such an expedition? And, even if one believes that there once was an actual Trojan War, does that mean that the specific events, actions, and descriptions in Homer's *Iliad* and *Odyssey*, supplemented by additional fragments and commentary in the *Epic Cycle*, are historically accurate and can be taken at face value? Is it plausible that what Homer describes actually took place and in the way that he says it did?

In short, the bigger picture involves the investigation of several major questions: What evidence do we have that the Trojan War actually took place? If it did, then where and when was it fought? What was its cause and who were the principal protagonists? What is the historical context into which the tale should be placed? Is there a kernel of truth at the center of the stories about the legendary deeds and actions of the Mycenaeans and Trojans, and do we need to bring other groups, contemporary to the Late Bronze Age, such as the Hittites of central Anatolia, into the equation?

The continuing mysteries, and the ongoing search for answers to these questions, keeps the modern investigation of the Trojan War lively and intriguing today, more than three thousand years after it presumably took place. Therefore, despite the beautiful simplicity of the tale, a book about the Trojan War is not as simple as it might at first appear. It will by necessity be far more detail-oriented and complex than one might expect, for the retelling of Homer's story is just the tip of the proverbial iceberg. Both Greek and Hittite sources document more than one Trojan War, so that one has to decide which is Homer's war, if any. Furthermore, since there are nine cities, built one on top of another, at the site of Hisarlik (ancient Troy), one has to decide which one was Priam's, if any. But before proceeding to these discussions, it is imperative to go through the story itself and ascertain what we know about the Trojan War from the Greek sources.

Part I
The Trojan War

Chapter 1

The story according to the *Iliad*, the *Odyssey*, and the *Epic Cycle*

The story of the Trojan War is well known, especially to those who were assigned to read the *Iliad* or the *Odyssey* in high school or college, or who have read one or more of the numerous translations that have appeared in recent years or seen the Hollywood movie *Troy*. Surprisingly, despite their length and detail, neither the *Iliad* nor the *Odyssey* emphasize many of the events with which the modern reader is familiar, including a fateful encounter on a hillside in ancient Turkey, the capture of Troy using the stratagem of a hollow wooden horse, and the subsequent journeys of the Greek warriors, apart from Odysseus, back to their homes across the sea. The Trojan Horse, for example, is mentioned only once in the *Odyssey*, within Book IV, when Menelaus is describing his travels and travails. It is not mentioned at all in the *Iliad*.

For the full story of the Trojan War and its aftermath, we must turn to the group of twelve epic narratives now known collectively as the *Epic Cycle*, which most likely date to the eighth to sixth centuries BCE, the approximate time of Homer and shortly thereafter. The *Iliad* and the *Odyssey* are the only complete works remaining from this group. The rest of these early epic poems were mostly lost over the course of time, and only portions remain, quoted or summarized by later authors. These literary fragments were gathered together by an individual who identified himself as Proclus—now thought by some scholars to be Eutychius Proclus, a grammarian and tutor of the Roman emperor Marcus Aurelius who lived during the second century CE. Alternatively, some attribute the collection to an individual named Proclus who was versed in the philosophy of Plato (a "Neoplatonist") and who lived three hundred years later, during the fifth century CE.

In any event, one or the other Proclus published these brief summaries and snippets of quotations from the various epics in a book called the *Chrestomatheia Grammatiki*. Its title derives from the Greek words meaning "useful to learning" and from which comes our modern word "chrestomathy," frequently defined as "a selection of choice literary passages from one or more authors." In uniting these fragmentary epics, Proclus created what now appears to be a seamless tale out of what were once disparate stories.

The literary fragments of the other epics expand on the sometimes-sparse details given by Homer. When gathered together, they provide information on the origins of the Trojan War. They also describe a first failed attempt by the Greeks to take Troy, and they give a complete account of the Trojan Horse. Later treatments of the story by the playwrights of Classical Greece in the fifth century BCE, as well as alternative versions, expansions, and continuations of the saga by much later writers including Virgil, Ovid, Livy, and Quintus Smyrnaeus, add still more details and flesh out the story into the form that we now know today. Not surprisingly, these later additions frequently contradict the original storyline, including details such as whether Helen was actually at Troy during the war.

The *Cypria*

The *Epic Cycle* begins with the *Cypria*, which was initially eleven books (or chapters) long and covered both the events leading up to the Trojan War and the first nine years of the war. Only a lengthy, but useful, summary of the *Cypria* still survives. Proclus tells us that the original author was not Homer but either a man named Hegesias, reportedly from the island of Salamis, or one named Stasinus, supposedly from Cyprus. A different tradition holds that the epic was actually written by Cyprias of Halicarnassus (on the western coast of Turkey) and that the title derives from his name. All three possible authors of the text probably lived during the sixth century BCE.

At the outset of the *Cypria*, we are told that Zeus—for reasons that are not specified—plotted to begin the Trojan War. To this end, he sent the goddess of Strife, Eris, to the wedding of Peleus, a war-hero and royal prince from the island of Aegina, and Thetis, a sea nymph. They would later become the parents of the as-yet-unborn hero Achilles.

At their wedding, Eris induced an argument between Hera (wife of Zeus), Athena (goddess of wisdom and war), and Aphrodite (goddess of love and beauty), as to which one of them was the most beautiful. Later sources elaborate upon this story, stating that Eris deliberately started the quarrel by throwing a golden apple, inscribed "for the most beautiful," into the crowd of guests. Hera, Athena, and Aphrodite, each one believing that it was meant for herself, could not settle the dispute by themselves. Therefore, Zeus ordered the messenger god Hermes to lead the three goddesses to Mount Ida, in what is now western Turkey (ancient Anatolia), where they came upon a young man.

The text identifies the young man as Alexander, while a note made by a later commentator in the margin of one of the earliest extant editions indicates that this Alexander, who appears here in the

Epic Cycle for the first time, is specifically to be equated with Paris. Although Homer and the early Greek poets refer to him far more often as Alexander, modern audiences know him better as Paris, perhaps to avoid confusion with the later Alexander the Great, who was not yet alive at the time that Homer was writing. Here Alexander/Paris is described as the "fairest of mortals," who agrees to decide among the three goddesses, in what is now known as the "Judgment of Paris." The painting by that name by Peter Paul Rubens provides a striking visual image of what is said to have happened on Mount Ida.

Although Alexander/Paris was the son of Priam, king of Troy, he had been banished from the royal court as a new-born infant. Apparently, Priam had a dream in which his wife Hecuba gave birth not to a son but to a torch of flaming snakes. Sparks from the torch lit the tall grass surrounding the city of Troy on fire and burned the city to the ground. When Priam summoned the dream interpreters, they declared that the unborn child would be a curse upon the city and to his father. They recommended that he be left in the forest to die, so that the prophecy might not come to pass.

As soon as he was born, the child was given to Priam's herdsman, who took the infant to Mount Ida and left him out in the open to die. He was saved, however, by a bear, which nurtured him until the herdsman returned and found the boy still alive. The herdsman then took the boy home and raised him as his own son.

When making his great decision as to who was the most beautiful of the three goddesses, Alexander/Paris was unaware that he himself was of royal birth. It was only later that he went to Troy, discovered his true identity, and was reunited with his father, mother, and entire family. It may be for this reason that he has two names: the one given to him either at birth or after rejoining his family and the one given to him by the herdsman. There are, of course, numerous other possible explanations for his two names, including that one was used by the Trojans and the other by the Greeks or that we are seeing here the conflation of two myths or legends that were originally separate, one featuring someone named Paris and the other Alexander.

This latter suggestion—that what we are seeing here is the result of the merging of similar stories—seems perhaps most likely, for it has been pointed out that there are numerous instances of duplicate, and even triplicate, names found in these epics; not only two names for Alexander/Paris but also two names for the major river near Troy (Skamandros and Xanthos) and fully three names for the Mycenaeans (Achaeans, Danaans, and Argives). We may note the duplication readily in his case, since, for example, he is called both Alexander (Ἀλέξανδρος) and Paris (Πάριος and Πάρις) even within Book III of the *Iliad* (compare lines 16 and 30 with lines 325 and 437). Overall, within the *Iliad*, he is called Paris in seven books and Alexander in five books; he is also referred to by both names in the *Epic Cycle*.

As for the city itself, it also has two names. Although Homer and all other authors always called the inhabitants Trojans, the city in which they live is called Troy (Τροίη) once and Ilios (" Ιλιον or 'Ιλίου) six times in the *Epic Cycle*. Homer also uses the two terms interchangeably; in the *Iliad*; for instance, he calls the city both Ilios and Troy already within Book I (compare lines 71 and 129). Scholars have long known that the name Ilios was originally written with an initial digamma in Greek, meaning that it was spelled and meant to be pronounced with a "W" at the beginning, thus "(W)ilios" rather than simply "Ilios." Over time, the initial digamma was lost, leaving the name of the city simply as Ilios.

In any event, this rather unbelievable story is known as a "foundation myth," commonly used in antiquity to describe and explain the rise of someone unexpected to the throne of a country or the leadership of a people. The best-known examples from elsewhere in the ancient world, including both legendary and historical figures, are Sargon the Great of Akkad in Mesopotamia during the twenty-third century BCE; Moses in Egypt during the thirteenth century BCE; Romulus and Remus in Italy during the eighth century BCE; and particularly Cyrus the Great of Persia during the sixth century BCE. Each of these stories resembles that of Alexander/Paris to a certain degree.

According to the *Cypria*, and as repeated in other ancient Greek myths and writings, Alexander/Paris chose Aphrodite as the winner of the beauty contest between the three goddesses after she promised him that he would win the love of, and marry, Helen—described elsewhere as the most beautiful woman in the world. The bribes offered by the other two goddesses, wisdom from Athena, and wealth and power from Hera, were apparently not as appealing as the prospect of marrying the beautiful Helen.

The *Cypria* then skips over the reuniting of Alexander/Paris with his family and his move back to Troy, and resumes with his voyage across the Aegean to the Greek mainland. There he is entertained by the Mycenaean king of Sparta, Menelaus, and his beautiful wife, Helen.

Menelaus was either very trusting or not very bright, for he left for Crete soon after Alexander/Paris's arrival. It is not made clear in the *Cypria* why he departed, despite the fact that he was still entertaining Alexander/Paris and his entourage. And why did he not take Helen with him to Crete? The summary merely says— very discreetly—that while Menelaus was gone, "Aphrodite brings Helen and Alexandrus [Alexander/Paris] together, and they, after their union, put very great treasures on board and sail away by night." Of course, the Greeks claimed that she had been kidnapped, whereas the Trojans claimed that she had left willingly with Alexander/Paris. In any event, Menelaus had every right to sue for "alienation of affection"; either that, or go to war with the Greeks and win her back.

This may not have been the first time that Helen was "kidnapped." A later Greek author, Athenaeus of Naucratis, who lived and wrote ca. 300 CE, reports that she had earlier also been kidnapped, as a young girl, by the hero Theseus, who is perhaps better known for having made off with Ariadne, daughter of King Minos, after killing the minotaur (half man/half bull) on Crete.

Interestingly, the *Cypria* does not say that Alexander/Paris and Helen went straight to Troy but rather that Hera, still miffed by her rejection, stirred up a storm against them, so that their ship was carried to Sidon, in what is now Lebanon. Instead of simply disembarking, Alexander/Paris interrupted his dalliance with Helen long enough to attack and capture the city. Only then did the two lovebirds continue on and return to Troy. Homer agrees, in the *Iliad*, that they stopped off at Sidon before reaching Troy, saying:

> There lay the elaborately wrought robes, the work of Sidonian women, whom Alexandros [Alexander/Paris] himself, the godlike, had brought home from the land of Sidon, crossing the wide sea, on that journey when he brought back also gloriously descended Helen. (*Il.* VI.289–92)

In any event, the *Cypria*'s brief mention of the attack against Sidon is not further explained. Herodotus, the fifth century BCE Greek historian, knew of the version presented in the *Cypria*, for he makes reference to it and notes that Homer knew of it as well, quoting as proof the lines given above. His argument is not very convincing, since Homer gives no indication that the visit was at all hostile. However, Herodotus also relates at length an alternative version of the story, in which Alexander/Paris and Helen were blown off course and landed in Egypt rather than Lebanon (*Histories* II.113–18). At this point, the plot gets a bit murky, since a similar story line was followed by the Greek playwright Euripides. He says in his play *Helen*, produced in 412 BCE, that the real Helen was whisked away by Hera and spent ten years in

Egypt, having been replaced by a phantom look-alike who went with Alexander/Paris to Troy.

According to the *Cypria*, when Menelaus heard what had happened, he returned home and planned an expedition to Troy with his brother, Agamemnon, the king of Mycenae, in order to regain Helen. He then traveled around the Greek mainland, recruiting Nestor, the king of Pylos, and Odysseus, who pretended at first to be insane and only later reluctantly agreed to take part in the mission. No mention is given in the summary of the other Greek leaders and men who also agreed to participate, but a full list is given in the so-called Catalogue of Ships in the *Iliad* (*Il.* II. 494–759). Here the various Mycenaean kings and the ships and men that they each brought are enumerated; Christopher Marlowe summarized their numbers well in *Doctor Faustus*, when he wrote of Helen:

> Was this the face that launch'd a thousand ships
> And burnt the topless towers of Ilium?
> Sweet Helen, make me immortal with a kiss.

According to the account in the *Cypria*, the Mycenaean ships, and the men upon them, then gathered together at Aulis, a port city on the eastern coast of Boeotia in mainland Greece, where they made sacrifices to the gods and then set out for Troy. Unfortunately, in one of those unpredictable misfortunes of war, they instead landed at a place called Teuthrania, located to the south of Troy on the Anatolian mainland, mistook it for Troy, and destroyed it. Before they could rectify their error and attack Troy itself, a storm hit and scattered their ships. They had to regroup at Aulis an unspecified time later—perhaps as much as nine years later, according to an interesting suggestion made by German scholars studying these *Epic Cycle* fragments. A nine-year delay would explain why the entire Trojan War took ten years, but only a portion of the last year of fighting is described in the *Iliad*.

It is while they were waiting to set sail from Aulis for the second time that a tragic series of events, immortalized by the later Greek playwrights, took place. Because the goddess Artemis, for reasons best known to herself, had sent winds that prevented the fleet from sailing, the increasingly impatient Agamemnon took measures that we would regard as rather extreme. He planned to sacrifice his own daughter Iphigenia in order to placate the goddess. The *Cypria*, however, puts a pleasant spin on these events, stating that Artemis snatched Iphigenia away at the last minute, making her immortal, and left a stag on the altar in her place, much as Isaac was replaced by a ram during the intended sacrifice by Abraham, as related in Genesis 22 of the Hebrew Bible. Euripides's play, *Iphigenia at Aulis*, produced around 410 BCE, follows the same scenario in replacing Iphigenia with a deer. But other authors, such as the slightly earlier fifth-century BCE Greek playwright Aeschylus, have her actually sacrificed, as seen in his play *Agamemnon*, produced in 458 BCE.

In any event, the expedition eventually set sail again, first to the island of Tenedos, then to the island of Lemnos, and finally reached Troy on the Anatolian coast. This time they attacked the correct city. But the attack failed and the Greeks were driven back by the Trojans. This event, its protagonists, and what follows is described succinctly in the *Cypria*; it is worth quoting in detail:

> Then the Greeks tried to land at Ilium, but the Trojans prevent them, and Protesilaus is killed by Hector. Achilles then kills Cycnus, the son of Poseidon, and drives the Trojans back. The Greeks take up their dead and send envoys to the Trojans demanding the surrender of Helen and the treasure with her. The Trojans refusing, they first assault the city, and then go out and lay waste the country and cities round about. After this, Achilles desires to see Helen, and Aphrodite and Thetis contrive a meeting between them. The Achaeans next desire to return home, but are restrained by Achilles,

who afterwards drives off the cattle of Aeneas, and sacks Lyrnessus and Pedasus and many of the neighbouring cities, and kills Troilus. Patroclus carries away Lycaon to Lemnos and sells him as a slave, and out of the spoils Achilles receives Briseis as a prize, and Agamemnon Chryseis. Then follows the death of Palamedes, the plan of Zeus to relieve the Trojans by detaching Achilles from the Hellenic confederacy, and a catalogue of the Trojan allies.

Thus ends the summary of the contents of the *Cypria*, setting the stage for the first book of Homer's *Iliad* and a quarrel between the Greek hero Achilles and King Agamemnon over their prizes of war. It is at this point that the *Iliad* fits into the series of poems that make up the *Epic Cycle*.

The *Iliad*

The *Iliad*, which describes in detail some of the action that takes place in the tenth, and final, year of the Trojan War, ends before the actual capture and sacking of Troy. The quarrel between Achilles and Agamemnon is the opening act in Book I and sets the scene for the rest of the story line. The quarrel arises because it is decreed that one of Agamemnon's war prizes, the Trojan captive Chryseis, daughter of a priest of Apollo, must be returned to her father. In order to make up for his loss, Agamemnon then takes Briseis, Achilles's prize from the earlier battle. Achilles, in turn, swears that he will not fight again until Briseis is returned to him and Agamemnon has apologized. Agamemnon refuses to do so, with the result that the Greeks lose the services of Achilles, their best fighter, albeit temporarily, but with disastrous results.

The story of the *Iliad* covers no more than fifty days during the course of the ten-year-long war. The information in the account is detailed and impressive, but uneven. For instance, Book I covers approximately twenty days, while Books II–VII cover only two days in a wealth of detail. In Book II, we are given an itemized description of the Greek forces—the Catalogue of Ships—followed by a similar but shorter description of the Trojan forces. Book III describes a one-on-one battle between Alexander/Paris and Menelaus, a duel with the winner taking all, including Helen, in a bid to end the war without further fighting. The war was not to be ended so easily, however, for Aphrodite rescued Alexander/Paris at the last minute. In the story, with Menelaus nearly victorious and dragging Alexander/Paris off the field of battle by the chinstrap of his helmet, Aphrodite causes the chinstrap to break, thereby saving him from certain death and ensuring that the war would continue. Books IV–VII are concerned first with events among the gods on Mount Olympus and then shift to the battlefield, with scenes of more fighting.

The next three books, VIII–X, are taken up with details of fighting during the course of a single day, including a long but inconclusive duel between Hector, Alexander/Paris's older brother, and Ajax, a giant Greek hero who would later take his own life. Eight books, XI–XVIII, making up one-third of the entire contents of the twenty-four-book *Iliad*, also consist of an account of a single day's fighting, presented in great detail. In part this is because Book XVI contains the events surrounding the death of Patroclus, Achilles's companion. Patroclus had borrowed Achilles's armor and was mistaken for Achilles as he fought throughout the day, only to be killed by Hector in the end. Book XVII describes the fighting over Patroclus's body, after Hector has stripped it of Achilles's armor.

The events of still another day take up Books XIX–XXII. By Book XX, Achilles has returned ferociously to the fight. The gods have now entered the fray as well, and Poseidon sends an earthquake to influence the outcome of the battles. In Book XXII, Hector is killed by Achilles, who then drags the corpse back to the Greek camp. Books XXIII–XXIV, the final two books in the *Iliad*, describe the actions that take place over the next twenty-two days, perhaps to mirror the twenty days of events covered in Book I. In Book XXIII, Patroclus's body is cremated on a huge funeral pyre and funeral games are held. Book XXIV, the final book of the

Iliad, describes Achilles's anger and grief. Despite misgivings, he is eventually persuaded to give Hector's body back to King Priam. Hector's body is then cremated in turn on his own funeral pyre, during a twelve-day armistice. And, with that final scene, the *Iliad* comes to an end.

The remaining events of the war are told in additional, but fragmentary, epics: the *Aethiopis*, the *Little Iliad*, and the *Iliupersis* (*Sack of Troy*), thought to have been written in the eighth and seventh centuries BCE. They are also covered in a much later work, dating to the fourth century CE, by an epic poet named Quintus Smyrnaeus (Quintus of Smyrna), who wrote a poem titled *Posthomerica* or the *Fall of Troy*, consisting of fourteen books (chapters) covering the time period from the end of the *Iliad* to the fall of Troy. Most modern scholars agree that Quintus probably used these earlier epics to compose his own work.

The *Aethiopis*

The *Aethiopis* picks up where the *Iliad* leaves off. Written by Arctinus of Miletus (a town on the western coast of Anatolia/Asia Minor/Turkey), perhaps as early as the eighth century BCE, at approximately the same time as Homer's writings, it consists of five chapters or books. The action begins immediately, when Achilles first kills the Amazon queen Penthesileia, and then kills Memnon, an Ethiopian prince who was the grandson of King Laomedon of Troy, predecessor of Priam, and therefore the nephew of Priam and cousin of Alexander/Paris and Hector. Both had brought armies to the aid of the Trojans.

Achilles is then killed by Alexander/Paris, aided by Apollo. Since we have only the brief summary of this epic, we are not told how Achilles was killed, but we know from other, later accounts—such as Ovid's *Metamorphoses* (12.580–619)—that he was shot with an arrow in his heel, the only place on his body where he was vulnerable. His mother had held him by the heel when she dipped him into the River Styx as a child, in order to make him invulnerable to wounding. Following a fight for Achilles's body, the Greeks brought him back to their ships, cremated him on a funeral pyre, and held games in his honor. Marring these events is a dispute between Odysseus and Ajax over the armor of Achilles, but this will not be resolved until the next epic in the cycle, namely the *Little Iliad*.

The *Little Iliad*

Proclus tells us that the *Little Iliad* was written by Lesches of Mytilene (a city on the island of Lesbos), in four chapters. He is usually thought to have lived and composed his works in the seventh century BCE. The epic begins with Odysseus triumphing over Ajax and winning the armor and weapons of Achilles. Following the resolution, Ajax committed suicide; an act that was later the subject of a play in its own right, written by Sophocles in the fifth century BCE. More fighting then takes place, and a number of deaths occur on both sides, including, most importantly, that of Alexander/Paris himself. He is killed by a man named Philoctetes, who later become the subject of plays written by Sophocles, Aeschylus, and Euripides. Following the death of Alexander/Paris, an otherwise-unknown man named Epeius built a wooden horse, following instructions given by Athena. It is noteworthy that this is the first time in the *Epic Cycle* that the idea of a wooden horse has been introduced.

The implication in the *Little Iliad* is that it is Epeius's idea ("Epeius, by Athena's instruction, builds the wooden horse"). This attribution is repeated in the *Odyssey* (VIII.492–94; see also XI.523–35): "But come now, change thy theme, and sing of the building of the horse of wood, which Epeius made with Athena's help, the horse which once Odysseus led up into the citadel as a thing of guile." Much later, however, Quintus Smyrnaeus gives credit for the idea to Odysseus, attributing to Epeius only the actual building of the horse:

The only one with a clever idea
Was the son of Laertes [Odysseus], who answered with this speech:
"Friend held in highest honor by the heavenly gods,
If it is really fated that the warlike Achaians
Should sack the city of Priam by means of trickery,
A horse must be constructed to contain the leaders,
An ambush that we will welcome." (Quintus Smyrnaeus,
Posthomerica XII.23–29)

The *Little Iliad* succinctly states what happened next: "Then after putting their best men in the wooden horse and burning their huts, the main body of the Hellenes sail to Tenedos [an island just off the coast]. The Trojans, supposing their troubles over, destroy a part of their city wall and take the wooden horse into their city and feast as though they had conquered the Hellenes." Later Greek authors, including Quintus Smyrnaeus (XII.314–35), usually put the number of men inside the horse at thirty (with some traditions upping the number to forty), and give their names, including Odysseus as the leader, Ajax the lesser, Diomedes, and Menelaus himself. However, the summary of the *Little Iliad* is brief and does not name even these, but instead comes to an abrupt end, with the story to be continued in the next epic, the *Iliupersis* or *Sack of Troy*.

The *Iliupersis*

The *Iliupersis* or *Sack of Troy* is composed of only two chapters, but it is full of action and brings closure to this phase of the epic tale. It was written by Arctinus of Miletus, the same man who had composed the *Aethiopis*. In this poem, we learn that the Trojans, even though they had already brought the wooden horse within their walls, are suspicious of it and debate what to do. Eventually they decide to dedicate it to Athena and "turned to mirth and feasting, believing the war was at an end." Some remain suspicious, however, and in Book II of the *Aeneid*, the Roman poet Virgil has Laocoön, the Trojan priest of Poseidon, warn his fellow citizens, "Trojans, don't trust this horse. Whatever it is, I'm afraid of Greeks, even those bearing gifts" ("Equo ne credite, Teucri. Quidquid id est, timeo Danaos et dona ferentes."). From this comes our saying "Beware of Greeks bearing gifts" and the idea of a Trojan horse as a computer virus, a plague of modern technology, particularly one that lets hackers in through a "back door" program installed surreptitiously on one's computer.

Laocoön's warning was prescient, for the *Sack of Troy* next reports that the Greek army sailed back from Tenedos under cover of night, while the warriors in the horse "came out and fell upon their enemies, killing many and storming the city." Priam was killed at the altar of Zeus, and Astyanax, the young son of Hector, was hurled from the city wall.

As a result of the Greek victory over the Trojans, Menelaus regained his wife, Helen, and took her to the Greek ships in preparation for the voyage home. After much additional killing and the dividing up of spoils, including female captives, the victorious Greeks sailed for home, not suspecting that Athena planned to destroy them enroute. At this point, the *Sack of Troy* ends, having presented the story of the Trojan horse and the Greek conquest of the city. It leaves the tale of the aftermath of the war to another epic poem, the *Nostoi* or *Returns*.

The *Nostoi*

According to Proclus, the five chapters of the *Returns* were written by Agias of Troezen, whom other sources date to the seventh or sixth century BCE. Troezen was a small town on the Greek mainland that also happens to be the hometown of the legendary hero Theseus. The *Returns* is the story of how the various Greek heroes, apart from Odysseus, made their way back home to their lands and kingdoms across the Aegean Sea.

In the *Returns*, both Nestor, the king of Pylos, and Diomedes, king of Argos and nephew of Heracles, reach home without incident. However, Menelaus, who had argued with Agamemnon about when to leave Troy, was caught in a storm while sailing home. He reached Egypt with only five ships left in his fleet. We are told nothing more of this in the *Returns*, but Homer in the *Odyssey* (III.299–304) fleshes out the story, including having Menelaus later tell Telemachus that he subsequently wandered for eight years in the Eastern Mediterranean, visiting Cyprus, Phoenicia, Ethiopia, and Sidon, in addition to Egypt, before continuing his journey home to Sparta: "For of a truth after many woes and wide wanderings I brought my wealth home in my ships and came in the eighth year. Over Cyprus and Phoenicia I wandered, and Egypt, and I came to the Ethiopians and the Sidonians and the Erembi, and to Libya, where the lambs are horned from their birth" (*Od.* IV.80–85).

Agamemnon, on the other hand, initially remained at Troy in order to appease Athena, and then finally sailed home, only to be murdered, along with his companions, by his own wife Clytemnestra and her lover Aegisthus. This episode, and the subsequent events involving his two children, Orestes and Electra, were greatly expanded upon by the later Greek playwrights of the fifth century BCE, including Aeschylus, Sophocles, and Euripides. The book ends with a brief mention that Menelaus finally returned home, presumably with Helen, only after the murder of Agamemnon.

The *Odyssey*

Homer's *Odyssey*, the only other complete epic from the *Cycle* that is extant, follows in sequence after the *Returns*. It is primarily concerned with the travels and travails of Odysseus, in his ten-year attempt to return home after the conclusion of the war. Like the *Iliad*, the *Odyssey* is composed of twenty-four books (or chapters).

The story is well known, having been told and retold in various forms down through the ages.

Odysseus's journey is essentially irrelevant to the tale of the Trojan War, but the epic does on occasion give him, or one of his comrades, the opportunity to reflect back upon the years of war and to give additional details that flesh out the picture presented only briefly in the summaries of the other epics. In the end, after many adventures, Odysseus was able to reach his home and, with the help of his son Telemachus, killed all of the suitors who had flocked around his wife, Penelope. He then resumed his role as king over the island of Ithaca.

The *Telegony*

After the *Odyssey* comes the final book in the *Epic Cycle*, the *Telegony*. Consisting of only two chapters, it was written by Eugammon of Cyrene, according to Proclus. Cyrene was a Greek colony founded in the seventh century BCE in what is now modern Libya. Eugammon is thought to have composed this work, essentially a postscript to the *Odyssey*, just a relatively short time later, in the sixth century BCE. It begins with the burial of Penelope's suitors and ends with the death of Odysseus at the hands of Telegonus, his other son, whom Odysseus had sired during a year of living with the goddess Circe while enroute home after the war.

Later authors

The later Greek playwrights, as well as Roman authors such as Ovid, Livy, and Virgil, continued to expand upon the details found in the *Epic Cycle*, especially on the events that took place in the aftermath of the war. The details found in the earlier epics may be more trustworthy than those in later works, since they are closer to the action of the Trojan War. But the reader should be aware that even these early epics were not written down until at least five hundred years after the original war, in the eighth century BCE, and may not have been formalized until two hundred years beyond that, in the sixth century BCE. The accuracy of their details is therefore of concern both to Homeric scholars and Bronze Age Aegean archaeologists, as is the question of whether Homer himself actually existed and was the author of both the *Iliad* and the *Odyssey*.

Chapter 2

The Trojan War in context: Mycenaeans, Hittites, Trojans, and Sea Peoples

If the Trojan War did take place, both ancient and modern scholars agree that it was fought toward the end of the Late Bronze Age, near the end of the second millennium BCE. This was a time when the Mycenaeans of mainland Greece and the Hittites of Anatolia were two of the greatest powers in the ancient Mediterranean, with the region of Troy and the Troad (the Biga Peninsula in Anatolia) caught in the middle. Both civilizations flourished from 1700 to 1200 BCE; the Trojan War, if it did take place, had to have been fought before the demise of these two groups. Although the Trojans themselves are known only from excavations at the site of Hisarlik (ancient Troy) in northwest Anatolia, both the Mycenaeans and the Hittites are by now fairly well known. The other group that may have been involved, the somewhat shadowy migratory Sea Peoples, is less known but still intriguing.

Mycenaeans

When Heinrich Schliemann began to excavate at the ancient site of Mycenae on mainland Greece in 1876, little was known about the civilization that inhabited the region during the Late Bronze Age. Schliemann had gone in search of Priam's city of Troy in 1870, and having fairly quickly ascertained its location in northwestern Turkey, he was determined to find the palace of Agamemnon.

His excavations at Mycenae gave a name to the civilization, the Mycenaeans, and his work there, as well as at the nearby site of Tiryns, was soon supplemented by other early archaeologists of various nationalities, who located and excavated additional Bronze Age sites across the Greek mainland, on Crete, and on the Cycladic islands. Within two decades, it was clear that the Mycenaeans had been established on the mainland of Greece from ca. 1700 to 1200 BCE. The first definitive volume on this subject, *The Mycenaean Age: A Study of the Monuments and Culture of Pre-Homeric Greece*, was published in 1896.

Mycenaean civilization can be reconstructed not only from the material remains that have been found during excavations at sites like Mycenae but also from a series of clay tablets that have been recovered from most of the major Mycenaean sites on mainland Greece and even on Crete. The tablets are inscribed with a writing system, known today as Linear B, with the characters scratched into the surface while the clay was still wet. Linear B was successfully deciphered in 1952; it is an early form of Greek and was used predominantly by an administrative bureaucracy that required permanent records of inventories and commercial transactions involving lists of people and goods.

The largest number of Linear B tablets has been found at Pylos, legendary home of the old and wise king Nestor, which was excavated in the 1930s by Carl Blegen of the University of Cincinnati. The city, located in the southwest of the Greek mainland, was destroyed about 1200 BC—part of the larger series of catastrophes that brought an end to the Mycenaean civilization. The fiery destruction accidentally baked the clay tablets, preserving them where they fell, to be discovered and deciphered thousands of years later.

The texts inscribed on these tablets are not literary masterpieces but simple economic texts. They consist primarily of mundane inventories of goods either entering or leaving the palace, with line after line of the number of chariot wheels that need to be repaired, the number of bolts of cloth sent to Mycenae, the number of slaves who need to be fed. Some of the female workers listed in the texts found at Pylos have ethnic names interpreted as western Anatolian in origin. These women came from Miletus, Knidus, and Halikarnassus on the western coast of Turkey; others from the Dodecanese Islands located just off this coast. They were probably slaves bought or captured by the Mycenaeans in the years before the Trojan War.

The Mycenaeans had an economy that was based on the so-called Mediterranean triad—grapes, olives, and grain. It was a primarily agrarian lifestyle, based on farming with a little fishing thrown in, at least for most of the people. The higher classes were able to indulge in a bit more luxury, owning goods and objects made of gold, silver, bronze, ivory, and glass. A middle class of merchants, artisans, and long-distance traders sustained and provided these indulgences. A textile industry and a perfume industry were among the most profitable, as was the production of olive oil and wine.

Some of these goods—especially textiles, perfume, and olive oil—were in demand not only in Greece itself but as far away as Egypt, Canaan (modern Israel, Syria, and Lebanon), and even Mesopotamia (modern Iraq). Mycenaean pottery was also in demand both at home and abroad, although it is not always clear whether it was valued in and of itself or for the contents that some of the vessels held. Several thousand Mycenaean jars, vases, goblets, and other vessels have been found in modern excavations, stretching from Egypt to Anatolia and beyond, with more being recovered each year, including at Troy.

The palaces of the Mycenaean kings were usually built on the highest hills in each area or section of Greece, as befitting the highest levels of authority of the land. They were heavily fortified, with thick walls and massive gates at the entrance to the citadel, such as the so-called Lion Gate at Mycenae. However, these palaces were much more than simply the residences of the kings; they also served as storage and redistribution centers for goods created at home or abroad and for agricultural products gathered at harvest time for later use. Around the palace, contained within the fortification walls of the citadel, were also the houses of the king's courtiers, administrators, and family members, as well as the workshops of the palace craftsmen.

On the slopes of the hill, spreading out below the citadel of virtually every Mycenaean palace in Greece, were the houses of the lower city. Here and in the surrounding smaller villages lived the everyday farmers, merchants, tradesmen, and craftsmen upon whom each kingdom depended. The majority of these people, both men and women, did not know how to read or write; probably less than 1 percent of the population was literate.

The Mycenaean civilization came to an end ca. 1200 BCE, or shortly thereafter, as part of the general collapse of civilizations that affected the entire Mediterranean region at this time. The cause is still not exactly clear, but there may have been a combination of factors involved, including drought, earthquakes, and invasion by outside groups.

Hittites

The Hittites were a civilization known by name, because of the Hebrew Bible, but were physically lost to the modern world until their rediscovery in the nineteenth century CE. The Bible refers to the Hittites numerous times, primarily as one of the many Canaanite tribes, which also included the Amorites, Hivites, Perizzites, and Jebusites. There are also references to specific Hittites, including Ephron the Hittite, from whom Abraham bought a burial plot for his wife Sarah (Gen. 23:3–20), and Uriah the Hittite, first husband of Bathsheba (2 Sam. 11:2–27). King Solomon also had "Hittite women" among his entourage (1 Kings 11:1).

Eventually it became clear, after investigations by pioneers such as the Swiss explorer Johann Ludwig Burckhardt and scholars such as the British Assyriologist A. H. Sayce, that the Hittites were not located in Canaan but rather in Anatolia. One possible explanation for the Bible's erroneous location is that the original Hittites had disappeared by the time that the Hebrew Bible was written down, between the ninth and the seventh centuries BCE. Their successors—the so-called Neo-Hittites—were firmly established in the northern part of Canaan by that point, however, and it was they with whom the authors of the Bible were familiar and to whom they referred anachronistically. In addition, it also became apparent that the name "Hittites" is a misnomer. Because the Bible referred to Hittites, the term was simply adopted by scholars to refer to this Late Bronze Age Anatolian kingdom. The Hittites, however, never referred to themselves as Hittites; rather, they called themselves the "people of the Land of Hatti."

By 1906, German archaeologists had begun excavating at Hattusa, the capital city of the Hittites. Within a year they began to uncover clay tablets, which recorded aspects of daily life as well as official archival records and treaties. These were written in several different languages, including Hittite, Akkadian, and Luwian, all of which have now been deciphered to a large degree. All of the texts dated to the Late Bronze Age, for the Hittites, like the Mycenaeans, flourished from approximately 1700 to 1200 BCE.

We now know from those excavations and others at numerous additional sites throughout modern Turkey that the Hittites developed from smaller, little-known kingdoms into a fledgling empire in the mid-seventeenth century BCE, when they built their capital at Hattusa (modern Bogazköy, 125 miles east of Ankara). Some decades later they were already powerful enough to attack Babylon, bringing down the Old Babylonian dynasty begun by Hammurabi. Thereafter, until the collapse of the Hittite civilization in the twelfth century BCE, they rivaled Egypt as the main Near Eastern superpower.

We also know from documents found in modern Egypt, Syria, and Iraq as well as in Hattusa, that the Hittites traded, debated, and otherwise interacted with the other great powers of the Late Bronze Age. These included the New Kingdom Egyptians, the Assyrians, and the Babylonians, as well as smaller kingdoms at Ugarit and elsewhere in both north Syria and Anatolia, such as Troy (which the Hittites called Wilusa or Wilusiya). Overall, the Hittites seem to have been fairly self-sufficient, although we have textual evidence that they imported grain upon occasion, as well as probably olive oil and perhaps wine. After a century of excavation and study, scholars are now fairly confident about the reconstruction of Hittite society, religion, diplomacy, architecture, and material culture.

The high point of Hittite power came during the fourteenth and thirteenth centuries BCE, particularly during the reign of King Suppiluliuma I and the rulers who came after him, during which time the Hittite Empire expanded into northern Syria and came into repeated contact, and occasionally conflict, with the New Kingdom Egyptians. The last great Hittite king, Tudhaliya IV, who ruled from 1227 to 1209 BCE, claims to have conquered the island of Cyprus, carrying away gold and silver. The Hittite Empire collapsed soon thereafter, ca. 1200 BCE, perhaps because of the mysterious Sea Peoples who, according to Egyptian documents, destroyed the "Land of Hatti," or perhaps by unfriendly neighbors known as the Kashka, located just to the north of Hattusa.

Trojans

The region of Troy and the Troad was always a major crossroads from the Bronze Age on, controlling routes leading south to north and west to east, including the entrance to the Hellespont, the waterway leading from the Mediterranean to the Black Sea. Consequently, whoever controlled Troy also potentially controlled the entire region both economically and politically. It is not difficult to see why this region was so desirable for so many centuries to so many different peoples, from the time of the Trojan War right up to and including the Battle of Gallipoli during World War I. Thus, we should probably not be surprised that the Mycenaeans would also be interested in Troy and the western coast of Anatolia, especially since it was on the periphery of the region that they controlled in the Aegean, as well as on the periphery of the Hittite Empire.

Not much is known about the actual Trojans, though. Unlike the Mycenaeans and Hittites, who each had multiple sites in which their material culture and texts can be found, the Trojans occupied just one site, Troy, and its immediately surrounding area. Moreover, as scholars have pointed out, the Trojans were, literally speaking, anyone who happened to have been living in the city at a particular period in time. Since the city was destroyed and reoccupied several times during its history, with at least nine cities built one on top of the other within the mound of Hisarlik (identified as ancient Troy) in northwest Turkey, the ethnicity of the Trojans may well have been different in the third millennium BCE than it was a thousand years later, at the time of the Trojan War at the end of the second millennium BCE, and different again yet another thousand years later, when the Hellenistic Greeks and Romans occupied the site.

If we focus on the period of the Trojan War, however, we are able to glean some information not only from the four sets of excavations that have been conducted at Hisarlik/Troy over the past century and more but also from some of the texts found in other areas, belonging to civilizations dating to that time period. Thus, for example, we find Troy in the texts of the Hittites, assuming that we are correct in identifying it as the city that they call Wilusa. These show an ongoing relationship, sometimes hostile, sometimes peaceful, for several hundred years, with the Trojan kings frequently serving as vassal rulers to the Hittite Great King.

The Trojans were quite possibly also involved in the international trade that marked the cosmopolitan world of the Late Bronze Age. Numerous spindle whorls, associated with weaving, have been found during the excavations at Hisarlik, suggesting large-scale textile production. Homer also refers to the Trojans as breeders of horses, a valued commodity necessary for the chariots of the Bronze Age armies. However, both textiles and horses are perishable materials and little would remain of these in the archaeological record. Thus, we are hard-pressed to identify any Trojan goods that might have been exported to other parts of the Mediterranean at this time, including to the Mycenaeans, save for one particular type of pottery that has been identified as "Trojan Grey Ware," which may or may not have been produced in the Troad region.

Sea Peoples

We know of the Sea Peoples primarily from Egyptian records, for they attacked Egypt twice, in 1207 BCE during the reign of Pharaoh Merneptah, and again in 1177 BCE during the reign of Pharaoh Ramses III. They continue to perplex and mystify historians and archaeologists of the ancient Mediterranean, for they seem to come suddenly from nowhere, cause widespread disruption, take on some of the greatest powers of the region, and then abruptly disappear from history. It is the Egyptians who call

them the "Peoples of the Sea," in inscriptions that describe them
as coming from the north, from islands in the midst of the sea.
Ramses III says specifically:

> The foreign countries made a conspiracy in their islands. All at once
> the lands were removed and scattered in the fray. No land could
> stand before their arms, from Khatte, Qode, Carchemish, Arzawa,
> and Alashiya on, being cut off at [one time]. A camp [was set up] in
> one place in Amor. They desolated its people, and its land was like
> that which has never come into being. They were coming forward
> toward Egypt, while the flame was prepared before them. Their
> confederation was the Peleset, Tjekru, Shekelesh, Denye(n), and
> Washosh, lands united. They laid their hands upon the lands as far
> as the circuit of the earth, their hearts confident and trusting: "Our
> plans will succeed!"

According to the traditional interpretation, the Sea Peoples
brought an end to much of the civilized world at the end of the
Late Bronze Age, ca. 1200 BCE, including the Hittites, Canaanites,
Mycenaeans, and Minoans, but were then in turn brought to an
end themselves by the Egyptians. The damage that they did during
their marauding wave from west to east across the Mediterranean
region was irrevocable.

According to more recent interpretations, however, the Sea
Peoples are seen as much more than simply raiding parties and
may actually have been more of a migration of entire peoples,
complete with men, women, children, and possessions piled high
upon carts pulled by oxen or other draft animals. Why they began
their movements is a greatly debated question; the most likely
scenarios involve natural catastrophes such as a prolonged drought
or even earthquakes back in their homelands. They also may not
have been responsible for as much of the damage observable at the
end of the Late Bronze Age as has been thought, but rather they
were only one of the many factors that caused the Mediterranean
civilizations to come to an end at this time. And, it is not at all clear

whether they attacked Troy or had anything to do with the Trojan War, although such scenarios have been suggested.

Literary warfare

Life was not always peaceful in the Late Bronze Age, nor were relations always friendly even between trading partners and neighboring civilizations. Especially during the years from 1500 BCE to 1200 BCE, there were a number of major battles in addition to the presumed Trojan War, fought either between the various great powers of the day or by them against lesser powers during periods of expansion. For instance, in addition to the battles against the Sea Peoples in 1207 and 1177 BCE, the Egyptians fought at Megiddo (biblical Armageddon), located in modern Israel, three centuries earlier, in 1479 BCE, against an army of Canaanite rebels. The battle ended in a decisive victory for the Egyptians, led by Pharaoh Thutmose III, and its details were duly inscribed on a wall of the Karnak Temple in Luxor, Egypt, making this the first recorded battle in history.

Similarly, the Egyptians also fought a major battle in 1286 BCE at the site of Qadesh in what is now modern Syria. This time they were led by Pharaoh Ramses II and were confronting the Hittites, led by King Mursili II. They were fighting over control of land in the region, in what was disputed territory between the Hittite Empire to the north and the Egyptian Empire to the south. The battle ended with both sides claiming victory and with a treaty signed by both parties. Copies of the treaty have been found both in Egypt and at Hattusa in Anatolia.

What these battles have in common is that although there is literary evidence that they took place, and no reason to doubt that they did, there is as yet absolutely no archaeological evidence for any of them. It can be argued that the same holds true for the Trojan War, for which we also have literary evidence but no definitive archaeological evidence (though even that may now be changing, depending upon how one interprets the recent finds from the site of Hisarlik). Thus, the Trojan War is not necessarily unique in the Late Bronze Age, neither in its occurrence in the first place nor in the literary manner by which its very existence has come down to us today.

Part II
Investigating the literary evidence

Chapter 3

Homeric questions: Did Homer exist and is the *Iliad* accurate?

Modern scholars studying the Greek literary evidence for the Trojan War are generally concerned with what is known as the "Homeric question." This actually consists of a multitude of smaller questions, of which the most relevant are: "Did Homer exist?" and "Does the information in Homer's *Iliad* and *Odyssey* reflect the Bronze Age (when the Trojan War took place), the Iron Age (when Homer lived), or something in between?" Although both questions are important, the latter has the more important implications for scholars studying the Trojan War, or excavating for the remains of Troy, or trying to re-create the world of the Bronze Age in the Aegean and eastern Mediterranean.

Homer

Not much is actually known about Homer or his life. The ancients held him in the highest regard as a bard—a traveling minstrel who sang of the heroic deeds of an age gone by—and he is still regarded as the first, and possibly the greatest, of the Greek epic poets. His genius reportedly lay in compiling, combining, and perhaps even ultimately writing down the story (or stories) of the Trojan War. One scholar, Barry Powell, has made the rather unusual suggestion that the Greek alphabet was invented so that the epics could be written down—that it was "invented by a single human being . . . to record the Greek hexameters of the poet we call Homer." Others have suggested that Homer may have created the epic poems but meant them to be passed along by an oral tradition, as had the earlier epics, until what we now know as the *Iliad* and the *Odyssey* were ultimately written down, perhaps as late as, or even later than, the sixth century BCE.

Assuming that Homer is a real person and the author of the epic poems, both of which are open to question, when and where did he live? Herodotus thought that Homer had lived approximately four hundred years before his own era, stating: "Homer and Hesiod . . . lived but four hundred years before my time, as I believe" (*Histories* II.53). Since Herodotus lived ca. 450 BCE, that would place Homer in the middle of the ninth century, ca. 850 BCE. However, after decades of discussion, scholars now generally place Homer about a century later, ca. 750 BCE, in part because one of his students, Arctinus of Miletus (composer of the *Aethiopis* and the *Iliupersis*) is said to have been born in 744 BCE (see Clement of Alexandria, *Stromata* 1.131.6).

Ancient Greek scholars, writers, and poets, among them Aristotle and Pindar, argued about Homer's origins. Some thought that Homer came from the city of Smyrna on the western coast of Anatolia (now Izmir in modern Turkey) and had worked for years on the island of Chios; others said that he had been born on Chios or on the island of Ios. In short, there has never been general agreement as to his origins. Indeed, there are many scholars who have insisted that he never existed, at least not as he is generally portrayed.

On the other hand, it has been suggested that Homer was not a single individual but was at least two people, Indeed, it was long thought, by German scholars in particular (among them Friedrich August Wolf in 1795), that the *Iliad* and the *Odyssey* were written by different people. At one point, a stylistic analysis of the texts by computer seemed to confirm this conclusion, but no general consensus has ever been reached. It has also been suggested that Homer was not a man, but a woman. Although the case for this hypothesis has recently been explored, the original suggestion goes back more than a century, to Samuel Butler, writing in 1897.

Perhaps most intriguing, and eminently plausible, is the suggestion that Homer was not a specific individual but was, instead, a profession. That is to say, there was no person named "Homer," but rather that one *was* a "Homer," a traveling bard who sang the epics of the Trojan War for his living. If so, then one or more of these professional bards may have written down the oral version of the story when a new writing system became generally available in the eighth century BCE. Overall, there is no shortage of suggestions, and books, about Homer. The simple answer, however, is that we actually know almost nothing about him, most importantly whether he actually wrote the two works, the *Iliad* and the *Odyssey*, which are generally attributed to him.

Bronze Age or Iron Age?

As for the second part of the Homeric question, we may well ask whether the information in the *Iliad* and *Odyssey* reflects events that occurred in the Bronze Age (1700–1200 BCE), the Iron Age (1200–800 BCE), or sometime in between. In order to answer this question, we must use information gleaned from the texts and compare it to information gained from archaeology.

We begin by testing the premise that the descriptions in the *Iliad*, the *Odyssey*, and elsewhere in the *Epic Cycle* are accurate representations of Bronze Age Greek society, and that they were handed down verbatim and without dilution by bards during the five hundred years between 1250 and 750 BCE. Could a single poet, or many poets, have accurately remembered, and transmitted, tens of thousands of lines of information over five centuries? What evidence, or examples, do we have that this might be the case?

Modern scholars using ethnographic analogies, such as Milman Parry in the 1920s, have documented that bards could indeed have accurately transmitted orally thousands of lines of epic poetry, for they recorded examples of modern poets and bards reciting and singing epics in Yugoslavia, Turkey, and Ireland. Clearly, it would have been no problem to accurately transmit such poems, especially if many of the lines or descriptions are stock, formulaic, and repetitive, such as "grey-eyed Athena," "swift-footed Achilles," and "rosy-fingered dawn."

The Catalogue of Ships from the *Iliad* (II.494–759), which mentions 1,186 ships in all, is considered by many scholars to be a reasonably accurate remnant from the Bronze Age, orally transmitted by generations of bards over the course of five centuries. Archaeological investigations have shown that many of the cities and towns listed in the catalogue as having sent men and ships were inhabited only in the Bronze Age and had long been abandoned by the time of Homer. Only ruins, if anything, would have been visible at these once-vital places during Homer's lifetime. Legends and stories could account for memories of some, but not for all; the only way for such a catalogue to be so accurate is if it had been composed at a time when the cities were flourishing, during the Late Bronze Age, and had then been handed down from bard to bard until finally inserted and written down as part of Book II of the *Iliad*. However, it is not a completely unblemished remnant from the Bronze Age, for there are cities present that should be absent and cities absent that should be present, if everything were strictly Bronze Age. Instead, it seems to be an amalgamation, with changes made over the centuries as the story was handed down orally by the bards.

Overall, the *Iliad* seems to be a compilation of details and data spanning the full range of time from the Bronze Age to the Iron Age. This may be expected, if changes and updates were constantly being made to the poem as it was handed down over the centuries, in order to keep it fresh and relevant. For instance, both Patroclus and Hector are said to have been cremated on funeral pyres following their deaths in battle (*Il.* XVIII.138–257 and XXIV.784–804, respectively): "they carried out bold Hector, weeping, and set the body aloft a towering pyre for burning. And set fire to it." Although the practice of cremation, rather than burial by inhumation, is much more typical of Iron Age Greece than of Bronze Age Greece, a cremation cemetery dating to the late fourteenth century BCE, in which the remains were buried in urns, was uncovered in level VIh at the site of Troy/Hisarlik.

In addition, the boars'-tusk helmets described in detail by Homer had gone out of use by the end of the Bronze Age. Boars' tusks from such helmets, and depictions of warriors wearing them, have been found at sites such as Tiryns on the Greek mainland, Knossos on Crete, and on the island of Delos, but they would no longer have been seen by the time of Homer, despite the knowledgeable description found in the *Iliad* (X.260–65):

> Meriones gave Odysseus a bow and a quiver and a sword; and he too put over his head a helmet fashioned of leather; on the inside the cap was cross-strung firmly with thongs of leather, and on the outer side the white teeth of a tusk-shining boar were close sewn one after another with craftsmanship and skill; and a felt was set in the center.

Similarly, the description that Homer gave of Ajax, and the large "Tower Shield" that he used is thought to be not only from the Bronze Age but from a period in the Bronze Age even earlier than the Trojan War:

Now Ajax came near him, carrying like a wall his shield of bronze
and sevenfold ox-hide which Tychios wrought him with much toil;
Tychios, at home in Hylde, far the best of all workers in leather who
had made him the great gleaming shield of sevenfold ox-hide from
strong bulls, and hammered an eighth fold of bronze upon it. (*Il.*
VII.219–23)

Such shields, and boars'-tusk helmets as well, can be seen in the
so-called Miniature Fresco painted in a house at Acrotiri on the
Greek island of Santorini, dating most likely to the seventeenth
century BCE, four hundred years before the Trojan War is said to
have been fought. Some scholars think that Ajax was a hero from
an earlier time, who was originally featured in another epic, now
lost, and was introduced into the *Iliad* as a character who would
already have been well known to the audience.

The Trojan hero Hector also wields a Tower Shield in one scene,
where his shield knocks against both his ankles and his neck (*Il.*
VI.117–18). Hector is also described as "complete in bronze armor"
(*Il.* XI.65). This, like similar descriptions elsewhere in the book,
is now thought to be validated by a discovery made at the site of
Dendra near Mycenae, which produced a full suit (panoply) of
armor reminiscent of Homer's description but dating to about
1450 BCE. This would make Homer's reference another example
of Bronze Age knowledge.

The more usual pieces of armor, including the leg greaves used by
the "well-greaved Achaeans" to protect their shins, are described
numerous times in the *Iliad* (e.g., III.328–39; IV.132–38; XI.15–45;
XVI.130–42; XIX.364–91) and also reflect Bronze Age items
rather than those of Homer's own time. The equipment is always
donned in the same order: greaves, corselet, sword, shield, helmet,
and then spears:

Patroclus was helming himself in bronze that glittered. First he
placed along his legs the beautiful greaves, linked with silver

fastenings to hold the greaves at the ankles. Afterwards he girt on about his chest the corselet starry and elaborate of swift-footed Aiakides. Across his shoulders he slung the sword with the nails of silver, a bronze sword, and above it the great shield, huge and heavy. Over his mighty head he set the well-fashioned helmet with the horse-hair crest, and the plumes nodded terribly above it. He took up two powerful spears that fitted his hand's grip. (*Il*. XVI.13–140)

Patroclus is also described in the *Iliad* as climbing the walls of Troy three times, only to be knocked back by Apollo each time. Homer's precise words are: "Three times Patroclus tried to mount the angle of the towering wall, and three times Phoibos Apollo battered him backward with the immortal hands beating back the bright shield" (*Il*. XVI.702–3). The implication is that the walls were climbable and, indeed, when archaeologists such as Heinrich Schliemann, Wilhelm Dörpfeld, and Carl Blegen excavated the remains of Hisarlik/Troy, they found that the walls of the citadel of Troy VI were at such an angle and with enough spacing between the stones that they could be readily climbed in at least one place. At the time that Homer was writing, these walls may well have lain buried deep under the surface, unseen for hundreds of years. It seems likely, therefore, that Homer's description is an accurate recollection of a Bronze Age fortification wall that had been covered over long before Homer ever lived. And yet, Homer seems to be describing the outer walls of Troy, rather than the walls of the inner citadel, so there is some degree of confusion present in his account.

Perhaps most telling is that Homer's warriors almost always use bronze weapons, despite the fact that during his own age the weapons were all made of iron. In the *Iliad*, few objects of iron are mentioned, which is consistent with the fact that iron was known but rare and valuable during the Bronze Age. In fact, one of the few iron weapons known from the Bronze Age is a dagger found by Howard Carter in the tomb of King Tutankhamun in Egypt, dating to the fourteenth century BCE, which presents a possible parallel

for the iron knife held by Achilles as he mourned Patroclus
(*Il.* XVIII.32–34).

Other details given by Homer confuse Bronze Age items and
practices with those from the Iron Age. These are primarily
minutiae, such as the number of spokes used in the wheels of the
chariots used by Homer's warriors and the number of horses that
drew those chariots. Bronze Age depictions, seen, for example, on
grave markers found in the Shaft Graves at Mycenae and on gold
rings found in other tombs at Mycenae and elsewhere, indicate
that chariots at the time of the Trojan War had four spokes in
their wheels, were pulled by two horses, and were used as moving
platforms from which to fight. Homer's descriptions, however,
indicate that his chariots had eight spokes in their wheels (*Il.*
V.720–23), were frequently pulled by four horses, and were used
as "battle taxis" to bring the warriors to the front lines, after
which they dismounted to fight on foot—all of these are known
characteristics of Iron Age chariots and fighting tactics, dating to
long after the Trojan War.

Similarly, Homer's warriors usually carry two spears, which
they used for throwing (*Il.* III.16–20, VII.244–48). This was a
common Iron Age tactic, whereas warriors in the Bronze Age
more often are shown with a long single spear, used for thrusting
close-range at an opponent rather than throwing long distances.
Such long spears are only infrequently described by Homer.
However, he does mention an eleven-cubit-long spear wielded
by Hector (*Il.* VI.318–20) and a single long spear belonging to
Achilles (*Il.* XXII.273). Homer also frequently describes one-
on-one fights or duels between major opposing heroes, designed
to enhance the glory of the individual warriors; for example,
Ajax and Hector (*Il.* VII.224–32) and Achilles and Hector (*Il.*
XX). He also describes infantry marching in close formation (*Il.*
III.1–9). Both the individual duel and the method of marching
appear to be Iron Age methods of fighting, rather than those of
the Bronze Age.

Additionally, Homer speaks frequently of weapons and other objects that are characteristic of the Mycenaean period as well as those that occur in the later Iron Age. He describes Mycenaean weapons like "silver-studded swords" (*Il.* XI.29–31)—that is swords with hilts riveted with silver or gold studs, such as have been found in the sixteenth to fifteenth century BCE Shaft Graves at Mycenae—as well as a scepter studded with golden nails (*Il.* I.245–46). He also describes Achilles's new shield (*Il.* XVIII.474–607) as made in a manner similar to the inlaid daggers that have been found in the Shaft Graves at Mycenae and elsewhere (using gold, silver, and a black gummy substance known as niello, inset into a base surface of bronze). All of these are proper Bronze Age artifacts. But Homer also describes Achilles's original shield (which was lost when Patroclus was killed in battle) as having a Gorgon face on it: "And he took up the man-enclosing elaborate stark shield, a thing of splendor. . . . And circled in the midst of all was the blank-eyed face of the Gorgon with her stare of horror, and Fear was inscribed upon it, and Terror" (*Il.* XI.32–37). Shields with such blazons, as they are called, did not come into general use until the Iron Age, reaching their peak usage during the Greek Hoplite phalanx warfare of the seventh century BCE.

In sum, Homer's recitation of the Trojan War and the minute details of the warriors, equipment, and fighting, as depicted in our version of the *Iliad*, contains a combination of Bronze Age and Iron Age practices. This amalgamation probably reflects the changes that were introduced into the original story as it was handed down over five centuries. Scholars, both archaeologists and ancient historians, are therefore very cautious about using the details provided by Homer when trying to reconstruct the Bronze Age in the Aegean. Indeed, it is partially this temporal combination, mixing different periods, that led earlier classicists to doubt that the Trojan War had actually happened.

However, one can obviously make the opposite argument. Homer's discussion contains much detail about the many objects and places that were only in use during the Bronze Age and that were not rediscovered until modern archaeologists began their excavations in the early twentieth century. It would not be surprising, therefore, if Homer's epic poems did reflect an authentic event that took place at the end of the Bronze Age, even if his account also includes some inaccuracies or details that were introduced during the centuries of oral transmission from one bard to another.

Neoanalysis

There is, however, one other point to consider, and that is the assessment by a number of scholars who argue that within the *Iliad*, the *Odyssey*, and the *Epic Cycle* are not only items from later in the Iron Age, but also people, places, and events that can be dated to earlier in the Bronze Age, that is, to before the thirteenth century BCE when the Trojan War is thought to have taken place. These scholars, who together comprise an informal grouping known as the German Neoanalysis School, argue that one can find bits and pieces of earlier epics that have been inserted into the Homeric epics.

For example, the first, ill-fated, Achaean expedition sent to rescue Helen at Troy, as recounted in the *Cypria*, reportedly resulted in Achilles and other Achaean warriors fighting in Teuthrania, an area in northwest Anatolia south of Troy, at some time immediately prior to the actual Trojan war. (Ancient and modern estimates for the elapsed time between the expeditions usually range from a few weeks to nine years.) The account of this expedition is seen by Neoanalysts as an excellent example of a pre-Homeric episode, most likely referring to an earlier "Trojan War." They also see the figure of Ajax, with his Tower Shield, as coming from a previous time and an earlier epic. The same might apply to the figures of Idomeneus, Meriones, and even Odysseus.

Neoanalysts and other scholars also point out that the *Iliad* itself mentions that the Greek hero Heracles sacked Troy in the time of Priam's father, Laomedon, using only six ships (*Il.* V.638–42): "Of other sort, men say, was mighty Heracles, my father, staunch in fight, the lion-hearted, who on a time came hither [to Troy] by reason of the mares of Laomedon with but six ships and a scantier host, yet sacked the city of Ilios and made waste her streets." (This previous expedition against Troy is depicted on the east pediment of the Temple of Aphaia on the island of Aegina, off the coast of Attica not too far from Athens.) At fifty men per ship, that would have been only three hundred men, which would have been a fairly small fighting force. However, an alternative tradition, mentioned by the later Greek authors Apollodorus and Diodorus, said that Heracles had eighteen, rather than six, ships under his command when he raided Troy, which would have meant that he had nine hundred men, a much more formidable army.

Clearly, there was a tradition in Greece, reflected even in the *Iliad* and the *Epic Cycle*, that Mycenaean warriors had been fighting and adventuring on the western coast of Anatolia for decades, and perhaps centuries, before the actual Trojan War, and that Troy itself may have been attacked by Mycenaeans almost a century before Agamemnon took on Priam. The ancient historian Moses Finley, in his book *The World of Odysseus* (1956), suggested that there were many "Trojan wars" during the Bronze Age.

The verdict

We are left with some fundamental, commonsense questions. Were the events and plot of the *Iliad* and *Epic Cycle* believable? Is it plausible that what Homer and the other epic poets describe actually took place and in the way that they say it did? Would an entire nation (or its ancient equivalent) really have gone to war over one person? Could Agamemnon really have been a "king of kings" who mustered so many men to retrieve his brother's wife? Was Mycenaean society of the Late Bronze Age really organized in that manner? And, what about the Trojan Horse—is it conceivable that such a machine was built and used successfully to end the war?

The answer to all of the above questions is yes. For instance, Homer's descriptions of the action, travels, battles, and other minutiae all ring true and the events depicted in the *Iliad* are believable, even if the arms, weaponry, and tactics come from a broad span of time, reflecting the oral transmission of the story over centuries. Furthermore, Bronze Age Greece was indeed split into a large number of what were essentially city-states, with each king ruling over a major city, such as Tiryns, Pylos, and Mycenae, and its surrounding region. And Mycenae certainly seems to have been more powerful and interconnected than the other cities of the time, especially if the foreign goods imported into the city and found by archaeologists are an indication of its international status.

It is unlikely that the war was actually fought because of Helen's kidnapping, even though that may have provided a convenient excuse. The real motivations were probably political and commercial, the acquisition of land and control of lucrative trade routes, as were most such wars in the ancient world. There are later historical examples, however, in which an action involving a single person was used as an excuse and catalyst to begin a war. The prime example is, of course, the assassination of Archduke Ferdinand that set off World War I. The war was probably destined to take place anyway, but the assassination served as the spark. A second example comes from the world of the Hittites, when the royal prince Zannanza, the son of king Suppiluliuma I, was killed by unknown attackers while on his way to marry an unnamed Egyptian queen in the fourteenth century BCE. His father used the death as an excuse to begin a war between the Hittites and Egyptians—a war that probably would have been fought eventually anyway, again for territorial reasons, which had nothing to do with the death of his son.

The Trojan Horse is among the least believable elements in the story, but even its presence can be explained. It is, frankly, unlikely that the Greeks would have built such a horse and hidden men in it; and it is even more unlikely that the Trojans would have been foolish enough to bring it inside their city. However, Homer and the other bards were poets, and as such, may be presumed to have taken some poetic license. It is not out of the question that the Trojan Horse represents some sort of siege engine, whether a huge battering ram, such as the Romans used in 74 CE to destroy the wall surrounding Masada in what is now modern-day Israel, or a tower from which the warriors could fight, like those depicted by Sennacherib in panels at his palace at Nineveh showing the siege of Lachish, just south of Jerusalem, in 701 BCE. It has also been suggested that the Trojan Horse is a metaphor for an earthquake that destroyed the city, for Poseidon was the Greek god of earthquakes and his symbol was a horse.

A final question relates to whether Homer was describing one Trojan war or several. The Greek epic tales document at least three Mycenaean attacks upon Troy and the region of the Troad during the Late Bronze Age; first, from the time of Heracles and Laomedon when Troy was sacked; then the mistaken attack on Teuthrania by Agamemnon and his men; and finally the battle for Troy as depicted in the *Iliad*. Which of these is Homer's Trojan War? Or are they all? Could Homer have telescoped these actions into a single great epic, a symbolic and poetic representation of numerous smaller conflicts that took place over several hundred years on the coast of western Anatolia? Indeed, there are additional indications, both archaeological and textual, that Greek warriors were fighting on the northwestern coast of Anatolia, and perhaps specifically at Troy, long before the thirteenth century BCE.

Chapter 4
The Hittite texts: Assuwa, Ahhiyawa, and Alaksandu of Wilusa

The Greeks recorded the Trojan War(s), but so too did the Hittites, located in central Anatolia. The Hittites controlled much of the region during the Late Bronze Age, from 1700 to 1200 BCE, all the way from the western coast where Troy lay to the eastern part of the country where Turkey now meets Syria. Clay tablets inscribed with texts in Hittite, Akkadian, and other contemporary languages have been found by German archaeologists at the capital city of Hattusa, located 125 miles (200 km) east of the modern city of Ankara.

Wilusa

Among these tablets are a number mentioning a city or area known to the Hittites as Wilusa, which was in frequent contact with the Hittite rulers over the course of at least three hundred years, including periods when the kings of Wilusa ruled at the pleasure of the Hittites, sometimes as puppet kings. It seems likely, according to most modern scholars, that the city of Wilusa is the same place that Homer and the Epic poets refer to as (W)ilios (that is, Troy). The Hittite archives contain details of at least four wars fought at this city during the Late Bronze Age. We even know the names of the kings concerned, including one named Alaksandu who was involved in a conflict dating to the early thirteenth century BCE and another named Walmu who was overthrown by an enemy force just a few decades later; both events took place during the same general time period as Homer's Trojan War and either or both could be related.

Beginning in 1911 and continuing until the present day, numerous scholars have suggested that Alaksandu is most likely the Hittite version of the Greek name Alexander. If this hypothesis is correct, one could tentatively identify the man known to the Hittites as Alaksandu of Wilusa as the same man known to the Greeks as Alexander/Paris of (W)ilios/Troy. If the two are not the same, then it would mean that two rulers with very similar names were ruling over two cities with very similar names at about the same time in northwestern Anatolia. Such a coincidence seems unlikely, and one can reasonably argue that it makes more sense to equate the two men.

Intriguingly, we also have the text of a treaty that was signed between Alaksandu, king of Wilusa, and the Hittite King Muwattalli II in the early thirteenth century BCE, in the aftermath of a war that was fought at Wilusa/Troy. We do not know which of the many battles fought at Troy might be referenced by this document, and so we cannot with certainty say whether the document supports or conflicts with the idea of the same individual playing a role in the literature of both cultures. We must, therefore, go back to a time before the thirteenth century war and then proceed forward in time in order to determine whether the battle described in the Hittite treaty is the same as the Trojan War described by Homer and the Greek poets. We are firmly within the realm of Hittite history here and have a wealth of detail available, even if the names are initially unfamiliar.

Ahhiyawa

We must first consider approximately two dozen texts discovered at Hattusa that mention a power and people known as Ahhiyawa. Scholarly quarrels about the identification of Ahhiyawa, and its possible relevance to the Trojan War, have now been ongoing for more than a century, ever since a Swiss scholar named Emil Forrer proposed that Ahhiyawa is a reference to the Bronze Age Mycenaeans, that is, the people whom Homer calls Achaeans (among other names). He went even further and identified specific people mentioned in the Hittite texts, linking them to Homer's warriors. For instance, Atreus and Eteokles of Homer were Attarissiya and Tawagalawa of the Hittites, in his view.

Others soon weighed in, including the German scholar Ferdinand Sommer, who in 1932 published a massive volume with all of the Ahhiyawa texts then known, with the primary intent of disproving Forrer's suggestions. The debate has continued ever since. It is now accepted by most knowledgeable authorities that Forrer was

3. **Hittite Anatolia, ca. 1500–1200 BCE.**

correct in identifying Ahhiyawa as the Achaeans (Mycenaeans), most likely those from the mainland of Greece. If so, we can say that we have textual evidence for Mycenaeans involved in fighting and conflicts on the western coast of Anatolia as early as the fifteenth century BCE.

If Forrer is not correct, however, and the Ahhiyawans are not the Mycenaeans, then we have no textual evidence from the Hittites for any contact whatsoever between the two most powerful groups living on either side of the Aegean, themselves and the Mycenaeans. This seems unlikely, though, for if this were the case, we would have an important Late Bronze Age culture not mentioned elsewhere in the Hittite texts (the Mycenaeans) at the same time as having an important textually attested Late Bronze Age state or kingdom with no archaeological remains left whatsoever (Ahhiyawa). It makes far more sense to simply equate the two, as most scholars now agree.

Madduwatta and Attarissiya

One of the earliest of the so called Ahhiyawa texts excavated at Hattusa dates to the time of the Hittite king Arnuwanda I but recounts an event that took place during the reign of his predecessor, Tudhaliya I/II, who ruled ca. 1450–1420 BCE. (It is uncertain whether there were one or two kings named Tudhaliya in this early period; hence the designation "I/II.") Known as the "Indictment of Madduwatta," because it concerns the activities of a Hittite vassal named Madduwatta, the text records the details of a direct engagement between the Hittites and a man named Attarissiya, described as "the ruler of Ahhiya" (Ahhiya being an early form of the word Ahhiyawa).

The text says plainly and without elaboration, that Attarissiya came to the western coast of Anatolia and fought against Hittite troops. We are told specifically that a Hittite officer named Kisnapili led thousands of infantry and a hundred chariots into battle against the forces of the Ahhiyawan ruler. We learn further that an officer on either side was killed, although there is no mention of the losses suffered by the regular infantry or the chariotry. This would have been nearly two hundred years before Homer's Trojan War. If one believes the numbers, the two opposing sides were substantial and were engaged in a real war, not merely a skirmish, for one hundred chariots was a large fighting force for that day and age.

Assuwa rebellion

Also among the texts discovered by the archaeologists at Hattusa are perhaps six that mention a rebellion in a region known as Assuwa—a region that can only have been located in northwestern Anatolia. This was a confederacy of twenty-two city-states that eventually gave its name to our modern geographical designation "Asia." It appears in the Hittite records primarily during the reign of the same Hittite king Tudhaliya I/II, during the latter part of the fifteenth century BCE.

At the time, Assuwa and its king rebelled against Hittite overlordship of the region, which had been established earlier. Among the twenty-two named members of the Assuwa coalition is Wilusiya, known to be an alternate name for Wilusa (i.e., Troy/Ilios). There is also a place called Taruisa, which appears on only one other Hittite text but here appears immediately next to Wilusiya. It also has been proposed as Troy or, more likely, the region of the Troad. If correct, it is interesting to note that these apparently alternative names for the same region in the Troad, Wilusa/Wilusiya and Taruisa, mirror the alternative names that the Greeks had for the same area, Ilios and Troy.

The Hittite records, specifically those known as the Annals of Tudhaliya, record that the Assuwa coalition began its rebellion as Tudhaliya I/II was returning from a military campaign against the west Anatolian polities of Arzawa, Hapalla, and the Seha

River Land, all known to lie on the western coast or immediately inland. Tudhaliya personally led his army against the coalition and defeated them. The annals state that ten thousand Assuwan soldiers, six hundred teams of horses and their Assuwan charioteers, as well as much of the population along with their animals and possessions, were taken back to the capital city of Hattusa as prisoners and booty. Included among these were the Assuwan king, named Piyama-Kurunta, his son Kukkulli, and a few other members of the royal family.

The order in which the events actually transpired is not completely clear, but Tudhaliya then apparently appointed Kukkulli as king of Assuwa, in place of his father, and allowed the coalition to be re-established, this time as a vassal state of the Hittite kingdom. Kukkulli himself then rebelled in turn, but this second attempt at revolt also failed. Kukkulli was put to death, and the coalition of Assuwa was destroyed. Thus the coalition was apparently rather short-lived, as a consequence of the intervention of Tudhaliya I/II. It appears to have existed primarily during the fifteenth century BCE.

Two additional points are relevant here. First, a bronze sword was accidentally found in 1991 at the capital city of Hattusa by a bulldozer operator doing repair work on a road leading into the ancient site. The sword has one line of writing on it, inscribed in Akkadian, the lingua franca of the day. It reads, in translation, "As Tudhaliya the Great King shattered the Assuwa country, he dedicated these swords to the storm-god, his lord."

Clearly, this sword was captured and dedicated by Tudhaliya after his victory over Assuwa, for such an inscription would have been carved on the blade only after the battle had been won. It is also clear that there was more than one sword originally dedicated, since we are told that "these swords" were dedicated. Most important, however, is that this is not a typical sword for anyone to have been using in Anatolia at that time, for it appears to be a type of sword specifically made and used by the Mycenaeans of mainland Greece only during the late fifteenth century BCE. The fact that it had been used, and captured, during the Assuwa rebellion means that either Mycenaeans themselves were also fighting in that conflict, against the Hittites, or that they had supplied weapons to, and been otherwise supportive of, the Assuwa coalition. This presents a unique instance of material evidence—as opposed to textual evidence—of Mycenaean involvement in a conflict fought in the region around Troy, fully two centuries before the date usually given to Homer's Trojan War.

Wilusa and Ahhiyawa

In addition, at least one city-state that belonged to the coalition, specifically Wilusa/Wilusiya, continued to exist for another two centuries. During that time, Wilusa not only interacted with the Hittites but was also clearly involved with the political entity known as Ahhiyawa, as well as with specific individuals from that entity, for among the twenty-eight known Hittite texts that mention Ahhiyawa or the Ahhiyawans are a few that specifically discuss their activities as related to Wilusa. If the Ahhiyawans are correctly identified as the Mycenaeans, as most scholars now agree, then we have textual evidence that Mycenaeans were involved in the affairs, and fighting on behalf of, the city-state of Wilusa (Troy), from the fifteenth to the thirteenth centuries BCE.

For instance, Mycenaean involvement with Wilusa in the Assuwa rebellion may be circumstantially indicated in a much later Ahhiyawa text, which is a translation into Hittite of a letter sent by the king of Ahhiyawa to a Hittite king, probably Muwattalli II, in the early thirteenth century BCE. Muwattalli, we know, ruled from approximately 1295 to 1272 BCE. The letter, which is partly concerned with much earlier events, was thought until recently to have been sent by Muwattalli to the king of Ahhiyawa, but has now been shown to have traveled in the opposite direction; as such, it is one of a very few letters to have been dispatched by an Ahhiyawan king to his Hittite counterpart.

The primary topic discussed in the letter is the ownership of a group of islands lying off Anatolia's Aegean coast, which had formerly belonged to the king of Ahhiyawa but had apparently been seized by the Hittites. Within the letter, we are told that sometime in the past a Hittite king named Tudhaliya had defeated the king of Assuwa and subjugated him. This matches the account found in the earlier Annals of Tudhaliya and is undoubtedly a reference to the Assuwa rebellion, so we know that the letter refers to events that had taken place about 150 years earlier.

The letter is damaged and incomplete, but it now seems, based on a new translation, that a diplomatic marriage had taken place between the current Ahhiyawan king's great-grandfather and an Assuwan princess, at a time prior to the Assuwan rebellion, and that the islands were transferred by the Assuwan king to the Ahhiyawan king as part of the dowry. The Hittites claimed that Tudhaliya's victory over Assuwa during the rebellion had given them possession of Assuwa's offshore territories, but according to the letter's author, the current king of Ahhiyawa, the victory had taken place only after these territories had already been presented to Ahhiyawa. Now the Ahhiyawan king was, a century and a half later, seeking to reaffirm his claim to the islands through diplomatic means.

The new translation of this letter indicates that there were good relations and, most intriguingly, apparently a dynastic marriage between the Ahhiyawans and the Assuwans during the mid-fifteenth century BCE. If we are correct in our identification of Ahhiyawa as the Mycenaeans and of the Trojans (Wilusa) as part of the Assuwa coalition, then we have in this document a good indication of relations between the two regions, marital and otherwise, beginning centuries before the presumptive time of Alexander/Paris and Helen's illegitimate affair. However, the letter does not indicate definitively that the Mycenaeans were actually drawn into the Assuwa Rebellion, as previous translations had possibly suggested, but the inscribed sword found at Hattusa does imply some sort of involvement, and a defeat suffered by the allied Mycenaeans and Trojans.

Additional Ahhiyawa texts, as well as pottery and other artifacts found on the coast of western Anatolia, indicate continued Mycenaean involvement in the region throughout the fourteenth century BCE. Still another series of texts specifically relevant to Wilusa date to the early and mid-thirteenth century BCE, approximately the time of Homer's Trojan War.

The Alaksandu Treaty and other Hittite texts

The first of these texts was sent to a Hittite king (probably Muwattalli II) by Manapa-Tarhunta, a king of the Seha River Land, located in western Anatolia just to the south of the region of the Troad. The letter, which is primarily concerned with the defection of a group of skilled Hittite craftsmen, specifically mentions a Hittite attack on Wilusa: "[Thus says] Manapa-Tarhunta, your servant: Say [to His Majesty, my lord]: [At the moment] everything is fine [in the land]. [Kassu] came (here) and brought the troops of Hatti. [And when] they went back to attack Wilusa, [I was] ill."

We do not know why Muwattalli and the Hittites attacked Wilusa at this time, early in the thirteenth century BCE. However, the treaty that Muwattalli subsequently drew up and signed with Alaksandu of Wilusa, generally dated to about 1280 BCE, makes it clear that the Hittites claimed control over the city and the region thereafter, just as they had in the time immediately following the Assuwa rebellion.

The Alaksandu Treaty, as it is called, outlines a defensive alliance between Wilusa and the Hittites. Here Muwattalli writes: "You,

Alaksandu, benevolently protect My Majesty. And later protect my son and my grandson, to the first and second generation. And as I, My Majesty, protected you, Alaksandu, in good will because of the word of your father, and came to your aid, and killed your enemy for you, later in the future my sons and my grandsons will certainly protect your descendant for you, to the first and second generation. If some enemy arises for you, I will not abandon you, just as I have not now abandoned you. I will kill your enemy for you."

It is this part of the treaty that is of the greatest interest, for here we are told by Muwattalli himself that he had, at some point earlier in his reign (1295–1272 BCE), come to the aid of Alaksandu and killed his enemy. This, we can conclude, is probably accurate information, since there is no reason for Muwattalli to have misstated or misremembered such current information, known to both parties. The question, however, is the identification of the enemy of Alaksandu, whose name or nationality—frustratingly—we are not given. Nor are we told any of the details regarding the circumstances surrounding this event. Instead, Muwattalli continues on and reiterates the mutual defense pact that they have in place.

In brief, we have evidence from the Hittite texts of at least two conflicts fought by Alaksandu, king of Wilusa, at some point immediately prior to 1280 BCE. In one, against an unknown enemy, Alaksandu was victorious, but only because Muwattalli and the Hittite army came to his aid. Although this is in the approximate era of Homer's Trojan War, we do not know for certain that it was the Mycenaeans who were the adversaries in this conflict. In the other, against the Hittites, he was defeated and forced to sign a treaty. Neither event is consistent with the story told to us in the *Iliad* or the *Epic Cycle*. Thus, however tempting it is to link Alaksandu of Wilusa to Alexander/Paris of (W)Ilios/Troy, we cannot conclusively link these conflicts and this treaty to Homer's Trojan War, unless we posit that Homer has his details wrong.

The Tawagalawa Letter

Of the two additional Ahhiyawa texts that have some bearing on Wilusa, the so-called Tawagalawa Letter is of substantial interest. It is thought to have been written by a king of Hatti, probably Hattusili III, who ruled ca. 1267–1237 BCE, but possibly by Muwattalli II, who ruled slightly earlier. We possess only the third, and probably final, tablet of this letter, which is concerned with the activities of Piyamaradu, a "renegade Hittite" who was actively involved with Ahhiyawa. The letter does not give the name of the king of Ahhiyawa, but it does give the name of his brother, Tawagalawa, who was apparently present in person in western Anatolia, helping to transport local rebels to Ahhiyawan territory. Numerous scholars, beginning with Forrer, have suggested that Tawagalawa might be a Hittite representation of the Greek name Eteokles—Mycenaean *E-te-wo-ke-le-we*.

Within this letter, the Hittite king attempts to put words into the mouth (or onto the tablet) of the Ahhiyawan king, asking him to communicate specific topics to someone (probably Piyamaradu). He states, quite specifically, "O, my brother, write to him this one thing, if nothing (else): 'The King of Hatti has persuaded me about the matter of the land of Wilusa concerning which he and I were hostile to one another, and we have made peace. Now(?) hostility is not appropriate between us.' [Send that] to him." A few lines later, he says again, "And concerning the matter [of Wilusa] about which we were hostile—[because we have made peace], what then?"

This is one of the only instances in all of the Hittite texts thus far translated, and the first since the time of Tudhaliya I/II, where we have a specific reference to a conflict between Hatti and Ahhiyawa. Even in the Alaksandu Treaty, Alaksandu's opponent is unnamed and may not be the Ahhiyawans. And, we do not know the scale of the conflict described in the Tawagalawa Letter. Trevor Bryce of the University of Queensland points out that the Hittite word used in this text can be translated as meaning anything from "outright war, a skirmish or two, or merely a verbal dispute conducted through diplomatic channels." Nevertheless, this may be evidence that there was another hostile exchange between the Hittites and the Ahhiyawans (that is, the Mycenaeans) around the time that the events described in the *Iliad* were taking place.

Walmu of Wilusa

Finally, the last textual reference relevant to this topic is a letter probably written in the late thirteenth century BCE by one of the last Hittite kings, Tudhaliya IV, who ruled from ca. 1237–1209 BCE. It is known as the Milawata Letter, because of its principal concern with the city of Milawata (Miletus) as well as with the continuing activities of Piyamaradu (see table 1).

In the letter, the Hittite king notes that a king of Wilusa named Walmu, who had been driven from his land by unnamed forces, was to be reinstated, probably as a military vassal: "Now, my son, as long as you look after the well-being of My Majesty, I, My Majesty, will put my trust in your good will. Turn Walmu over to me, my son, so that I may reinstall him in kingship in the land of Wilusa. [He shall] now be King of the land of Wilusa, as he was formerly. He shall now be our military vassal, as he [was] formerly." Clearly the treaty signed with Alaksandu was still in force, for the Hittites had sworn to help his descendants to the first and second generations. One might speculate that this final conflict, during which the Wilusan king lost his throne as the result of an attack by a rebel force, only to have it restored to him by the Hittites, could have contributed to the later understanding by Homer that the Trojans had lost the war.

A Wilusiad?

Speaking of Homer and the Hittites, it was Calvert Watkins of Harvard University who first suggested, at a conference on Troy and the Trojan War held at Bryn Mawr College in 1984, that

Table 1. Known Trojan (Wilusa) Wars from Hittite records

Event	Wilusa ruler	Hittite king	Approx. date	Result
Assuwan revolt, two phases	Piyama-Kurunta and son Kukkulli	Tudhaliya I/II	1430–1420 BCE	Exiled to Hattusa (father) and put to death (son)
Attacked first by enemy and then by Hittites	Alaksandu	Muwattalli II	1280 BCE	Aided, then defeated, by the Hittites
Conflict over Wilusa between Hittites and Ahhiyawa	??	Hattusili III	1267–1237 BCE	Resolved
Attacked by enemy force	Walmu	Tudhaliya IV	1237–1209 BCE	Deposed by enemy, but then reinstated by Hittites

certain other Hittite texts might contain the remnants of what he called a possible *Wilusiad*. This would have been, he hypothesized, another historical epic about the Trojan War but one written from the perspective of the Trojans or the Hittites rather than the Greeks.

The *Wilusiad* will have been written in Luwian, a language or dialect spoken throughout Anatolia at the time, but we have only two possible lines left to us. One of the lines, inserted and quoted in a Hittite ritual text, reads quite simply: "[and they sing:] 'When they came from steep Wilusa.'" This language is reminiscent of Homer, who refers to Troy as "steep Ilios" no fewer than six different times in the *Iliad*. A second line, found inserted in another Hittite text, may be reconstructed to read: "When the man came from steep [Wilusa . . .]"

Unfortunately, we have nothing more than these two possible lines at the moment. But this could change, as additional Hittite tablets are currently lying undeciphered in collections throughout Europe and the United States, awaiting translation by scholars.

Speculations

A number of these suggestions are based on scholarly speculation, such as equating Wilusa with (W)ilios/Troy, Ahhiyawa with the Achaeans/Mycenaeans, and Alaksandu with Alexander/Paris. All of these are plausible, to a greater or lesser degree, with the consequence that some have been debated by scholars for more than a century. None is completely out of the realm of possibility, and some actually seem quite likely. Needless to say, if all were to turn out to be incorrect, we would be left with nothing substantial to point to, which remains a possibility. The majority of scholars, however, currently favor some or all of the above equations, especially the correlation between Ahhiyawa and the Achaeans, which allows us to utilize the Hittite texts as textual evidence with potential implications for several Trojan Wars.

So which of these four or more conflicts recorded in the Hittite texts is Homer's Trojan War? Are any of them? At least two, and possibly all, of these wars seem to have involved the Mycenaeans (Ahhiyawa) in some manner. At present, however, it is uncertain which, if any, of these conflicts is the Trojan War, as recorded by Homer and the Epic poets, or whether the Greek poems are a reflection of what seems to have been more than several hundred years of on-again, off-again conflict between the Hittites and the Ahhiyawans (Mycenaeans)—a telescoping of numerous events into a series of epic poems about the "war to end all wars."

Since the jury is still out, we must turn to the archaeological evidence that indicates several attacks, which resulted in destructions at the city of Hisarlik, identified as ancient Troy, during the Bronze Age. There are nine cities located one on top of another inside the ancient mound, and so here too we must consider which, if any, was the one immortalized by Homer in his grand epic of love and war, as recorded in the *Iliad*.

Part III
Investigating the archaeological evidence

Chapter 5

Early excavators: Heinrich Schliemann and Wilhelm Dörpfeld

The story of the search for Troy is inextricably intertwined in the story of the nineteenth-century businessman Heinrich Schliemann who is frequently referred to, albeit inaccurately, as the "father of Mycenaean archaeology." Schliemann was a German self-made millionaire who was among the luckiest individuals ever to put a shovel into the earth. His is a success story, for, as a self-taught "amateur" archaeologist, he was the first to comprehensively excavate at the site that most scholars now agree is probably ancient Troy. He did this against all odds and against the general thinking of the academics of his day, most of whom were convinced that the Trojan War had never taken place and therefore that there was no such place as ancient Troy. Schliemann also successfully excavated at the sites of Mycenae and Tiryns on the Greek mainland, searching for Agamemnon and his forces.

But, according to recent research, Schliemann was also apparently a scoundrel who falsified his excavation journals and who cannot necessarily be relied upon concerning details of either his professional or private life. For example, in his archaeology, he failed to give credit to Frank Calvert, the man who led him to the site of Hisarlik—ancient Troy. Moreover, Schliemann may have completely made up his account of finding "Priam's Treasure," which is neither Priam's nor a treasure per se but rather a collection of valuable artifacts that dates to fully a thousand years before the Trojan War.

Schliemann's search

Schliemann began his search for Troy after retiring from his business enterprises as a millionaire at age forty-five or so. He claims to have been waiting virtually all of his life, since the age of seven, to begin his search and prove that the Trojan War had taken place. In the introduction to his book *Ilios: the City and Country of the Trojans* (1881), he recounts seeing a woodcut engraving of Aeneas fleeing from the burning city of Troy, with his aged father upon his back and his young son holding his hand, in a book that he received in 1829 as a Christmas gift from his father.

Schliemann told his father that the story must have happened, and that Troy must have existed, otherwise the artist could not have known how to engrave the picture. (Such is the logic and reasoning of a seven-year-old.) He then informed his father that he would find Troy when he grew up. It is a marvelous autobiographical story, and one that is still frequently told about Schliemann. Unfortunately, it probably never happened. The story does not appear in any of Schliemann's writings, including his private journals and introductions to other books, until after he had already discovered Troy and announced to the world that the Trojan War had indeed happened. The scholarly consensus now is that Schliemann made up the tale much later in life, for reasons known only to himself.

Schliemann made his money as a successful businessman, who earned one fortune selling indigo, tea, coffee, and sugar in the

Crimea, and another during the California gold rush in 1851–52. It was in California that he served as a banker/middleman in Sacramento, buying gold dust from the miners and selling it to the Rothschild banking family, via its representative in San Francisco. He bought low and sold high—and, some say, kept his thumb on the scales while doing so. He may well have left California one step ahead of the law, perhaps with as much as $2 million in profits, amid charges concerning the amount of gold dust that he was shipping.

Schliemann kept journals throughout his life, and his time in the United States in 1851–52 was no exception. Unfortunately for Schliemann, several entries from this period show that even his private scribbling cannot be trusted. For instance, an ostensibly eyewitness account written by Schliemann of a great fire in San Francisco in June 1851 is highly suspect, for it appears that the fire actually took place a month earlier, in May, and that Schliemann was in Sacramento, not San Francisco, at the time. Detective work by David Traill, a professor at the University of California–Davis, has now shown that Schliemann had simply copied a newspaper account from the front page of the *Sacramento Daily Union* verbatim into his journal, changing the story slightly by inserting himself into it.

Additional "invented episodes," as William Calder III of the University of Illinois has termed them, probably include an entry for February 1851, in which Schliemann records that he was in Washington, DC and visited for an hour and a half with President Millard Fillmore during an extravagant reception. As both Calder and Traill point out, although this is not entirely out of the question, it seems highly unlikely that the president would have met with an unknown twenty-eight-year-old German, even one who spoke fluent English as did Schliemann. As with the San Francisco fire, the account was probably culled from a newspaper article, into which Schliemann placed himself.

While living in Sacramento in 1851, Schliemann filed a statement of intention to apply for US citizenship, although it was not until nearly twenty years later, arriving in New York City in late March 1869, that he did finally apply. In order to obtain it, however, Schliemann had to persuade a man named John Bolan to swear that Schliemann had been living in the United States for the five previous consecutive years, and that he had been living in New York State for at least a year, even though neither was true. Bolan had to perjure himself, but it worked. Schliemann received his citizenship, just two days after he arrived in New York.

A few days later, in early April 1869, Schliemann moved on to Indiana, which at the time had the most lenient divorce laws of any state. There, he applied to divorce his first wife, Katarina, who was back in Germany and with whom he had had three children, two of whom had survived childhood. By the end of June, having lived in Indiana for all of three months, he had received the divorce decree despite the requirement to have lived in the state for a year. Most likely he had found someone to testify to that effect, as he had just done in New York.

In the meantime, Schliemann had already begun to devote his life to finding the site of ancient Troy and proving that the Trojan War had taken place. A year earlier, in 1868, Schliemann had visited Ithaca and then Mycenae in Greece, before continuing on to Turkey. There, after fruitless visits to several ancient mounds favored by many others as the location of Troy, including sites known as Bunarbasi and Balli Dagh, Schliemann befriended the American vice-consul to Turkey, a man named Frank Calvert. Calvert believed that he himself had already discovered Troy. In fact, he had bought a portion of the ancient site—a mound called Hisarlik—and had already dug a few trial trenches. Calvert was by no means the first person to think that Hisarlik might contain the ruins of Bronze Age Troy; the suggestion had apparently first been made back in 1822, the year of Schliemann's birth, in a book published by the Scottish journalist Charles Maclaren, who was a member of several learned geographical societies. Calvert offered to join forces with Schliemann. It was an offer Schliemann gladly accepted, for he had money but no site, while Calvert had a site but no money. It promised to be a worthwhile partnership.

Upon his return from the United States, in September 1869, just a few months after procuring both his American citizenship and divorce through unorthodox and possibly illegal means, Schliemann married Sophia Engastromenos in Athens. He was forty-seven; she was sixteen. They had two children, whom they named Andromache and Agamemnon—but that would come later.

In April 1870, Schliemann began to dig at Hisarlik, ignoring the fact that he had not yet received an excavation permit from the Turkish authorities. He dug again at the site in 1871, but it was not until 1872 that he began his most audacious attack on the mound. Cutting a huge trench some forty-five feet deep right through the middle of the ancient hill, Schliemann had his workmen dig as quickly and as deeply as they could, for he believed that a city three thousand years old would be buried far below. He and his men cut through layer after layer of ancient settlements, first one, then two, then three cities, and more. Eventually, with the help of his architect, Wilhelm Dörpfeld, whose services he engaged ten years later, Schliemann identified remains from numerous cities built one on top of the other; he thought that there were six cities, or possibly seven. It is now clear, after more than a century of excavation at the site, that there were actually nine cities in all, with additional subphases and remodelings belonging to each. At the time, neither Schliemann nor Dörpfeld realized that there were so many layers.

Troy II and Priam's Treasure

Schliemann was convinced that the "Burnt City," as he called it, was Priam's Troy. It was unclear to him at first whether this was the second city built at the site—Troy II as it is now known—or the third city. Schliemann initially thought it was the second city but, persuaded by others, including Calvert, he mistakenly identified it as the third city throughout his book *Ilios* (1881). It was Dörpfeld who showed him, just one year later in 1882, that he had been correct in the first place; it was indeed the second city, rather than the third. Regardless of the label, Schliemann felt that this was the city that the Mycenaeans had taken ten long years to capture, using the stratagem of the wooden horse. The excavations of 1873, the year that Schliemann discovered Priam's Treasure, only served to convince him even more that he was correct in his identification.

Schliemann's own account of the discovery of Priam's Treasure says that he was wandering around the excavation one morning at the end of May, keeping an eye on all of the workmen, when he suddenly noticed one of them uncovering a large copper object, behind which he could see a glint of gold. Schliemann quickly announced to the workers that it was breakfast time, even though it was far from it, and while they were eating, he called for his wife and "cut out the Treasure with a large knife" (see fig. 4).

Schliemann says that he and Sophia unearthed the objects, including bronze, silver, and gold vessels, jewelry, and other artifacts. They did so at great personal risk, according to Schliemann, for towering above them was a high bank of earth, which threatened to come down upon them at any moment. Sophia gathered the smaller objects together in her apron or shawl and carried them into the house, and Schliemann followed with the larger objects.

Once inside, they made a quick inventory, noting that the treasure included a copper shield and vase; various vessels of gold, silver, or electrum; thirteen spearheads; fourteen battle axes; daggers, a sword, and other objects of copper or bronze; and numerous objects of gold, including two diadems, a headband, sixty earrings, and nearly nine thousand smaller ornaments. They then packed everything up in several large crates, and arranged for them to be

4. Pieces from "Priam's Treasure" were displayed by Heinrich Schliemann after their discovery at Troy. They were eventually shown to be from the Early Bronze Age, rather than the Late Bronze Age, and were a thousand years too early to have belonged to Priam.

smuggled out of Turkey and across the Aegean Sea to their house in Athens. When both they and the treasure were safely in Greece, Schliemann bedecked his wife in the gold jewelry and took her picture, before announcing to the world that he had found Priam's treasure (see fig. 5).

Knowing that Schliemann was untrustworthy in his personal life sends up a red flag that we might not want to take his word at face value when it comes to his professional life, especially the details recorded in his excavation journals. It is now clear that there are many problems with Schliemann's account of finding this treasure, first and foremost of which is the fact that Sophia was not even at Troy on the day that Schliemann said the treasure was found. His own diaries record that Sophia was in Athens at the time. He later admitted as much, saying that he just wanted to involve her in his life so much that he wrote her into the story, thinking that it would get her more interested in what had become his life's passion.

More recently, the treasure has been the focus of much scholarly investigation. It is abundantly clear that it cannot be Priam's treasure, for Schliemann identified its findspot as within the Burnt City, that is, Troy II, which we now know dates to about 2300 BCE. In fact, the items found in this "treasure" look remarkably like other items of jewelry found across a wide swath of territory, from the so-called Death Pits of Ur in Mesopotamia (modern Iraq) in the east to the site of Poliochni on the Aegean island of Lemnos in the west, all dating to the same approximate time period, just after the middle of the third millennium BCE and more than a thousand years too early to have belonged to Priam, Helen, or anyone else involved with the Trojan War.

Moreover, many scholars are convinced that Schliemann made up the entire story of its discovery—not only placing Sophia at the site when she was not there but making up the very existence of the treasure in the first place. Though there is little doubt that

5. Sophia Schliemann, shown in Athens wearing the jewels from "Priam's Treasure," which turned out to be from a period more than a thousand years before the time of Priam and the Trojan War.

Schliemann did find all of these objects at Troy, there is a good chance that he did not find them all together. Instead, many believe that he may have made a series of smaller discoveries all over the site throughout the excavation season, but held off announcing these finds until he had accumulated enough to put them together as one big "treasure" that would amaze the world when he announced its discovery. Ironically, if Schliemann had not erroneously labeled these items as "Priam's Treasure," they would not hold nearly the value nor interest that they do today. But Schliemann was a master showman and he knew that giving the items this label, whether accurate or not, would draw the world's attention to his site and his claim to have found the city of Troy, as indeed it did.

Eventually, Schliemann sent the treasure to Germany, where it was displayed in the Berlin Museum until near the end of World War II, when it simply disappeared for nearly fifty years. In the early 1990s, the Russian government admitted that the treasure had been taken to Moscow in 1945, as part of what they considered to be war reparations; it is now on display in the Pushkin Museum.

Since Schliemann thought that Priam's Troy was the Burnt City, the second of the nine cities that he had uncovered at the site, he and his men had dug hastily through the cities lying above, especially in the early 1870s. During his later campaigns, in 1879 and in the 1880s, he was far more careful, and often took the advice of scholars, but still much of the material from these upper, and later, cities was simply thrown out. This, as it turned out, was very unfortunate, for toward the end of his life, convinced by Dörpfeld and by his own findings at Mycenae and Tiryns on the Greek mainland, not to mention other scholars, Schliemann finally admitted that he had been mistaken. Troy II was indeed a thousand years too early and it was more likely that Troy VI or Troy VII—the sixth or seventh cities—were those belonging to the time of the Trojan War.

Schliemann eventually understood this, because he discovered the same sort of Mycenaean pottery at Mycenae and Tiryns as he had previously found at Troy VI and VII, meaning that these levels all dated to approximately the same time period during the Late Bronze Age. Others, including Frank Calvert, had for years been pointing this out to him and to anyone else who would listen. Unfortunately, it was too late. Schliemann's men had already destroyed or thrown away many of the very buildings and objects for which he had been searching. He had not realized that the later Greeks and Romans had already shaved off the highest part of the mound in order to build the temples and other structures of their own cities. Thus Priam's Troy—because of the earthmoving efforts of the Hellenistic Greeks and Romans— was much closer to the modern surface than Schliemann had suspected.

Schliemann began preparations for a new campaign at the site, but before he could begin, he collapsed on a busy city street in Naples on Christmas Day 1890. He died the next day. His body was sent to Athens, where he was buried in the First Cemetery, a place of honor. A monument was placed over his grave, in the form of a small Greek temple with various scenes relating especially to the Trojan War and his excavations at Troy, Mycenae, Tiryns, and elsewhere, complete with an image of Schliemann himself holding a copy of the *Iliad*.

Dörpfeld and Troy VI

After Schliemann's death, Wilhelm Dörpfeld, his architect, took over as director of the excavations at Hisarlik, financed in part by Sophia Schliemann. He dug for two seasons, in 1893 and 1894, this time focusing on the ruins of the sixth city at Troy. First settled about 1700 BCE, Troy VI had undergone many renovations, resulting in at least eight subphases, which were eventually detected by archaeologists and labeled a–h, before its final destruction several hundred years later.

Although Schliemann had excavated much of the central part of the citadel at Hisarlik, he had left the outer edges untouched, and it was here that Dörpfeld spent most of his time, money, and energy. His efforts paid off when he uncovered a tremendous fortification wall sweeping around the citadel of Troy VI, made of well-built limestone and worthy of Homer's heroic epics.

Dörpfeld uncovered three hundred yards of this wall, as well as entry gates and a watchtower still standing to a height of twenty-five feet. It is the remains of these fortifications that can be seen today when one visits Hisarlik/Troy (see fig. 6). Homer may have been accurately describing them in the *Iliad*, complete with the angle or "batter" mentioned in connection with Patroclus's attempt to climb the wall (*Il.* XVI.702–3), despite his possible confusion between the inner walls of the citadel and the outer walls of the city.

The final version of this city, Troy VIh, was the most impressive. Not only were there the high walls and towers of stone surrounding the citadel, but large houses and the palace graced the interior. This was a wealthy city, a desirable plum commanding the Hellespont—the passageway from the Aegean to the Black Sea—and growing wealthier from a combination of trade and taxation. At certain points during this period, its wealth and foreign contacts may have rivaled that of the larger Mycenaean palaces, though perhaps not that of Mycenae itself. The winds and the current in the Hellespont frequently presented adverse conditions for ships wishing to sail up to the Black Sea, and so these ships presumably would be forced to linger, sometimes for weeks on end, until the weather turned in their favor. Troy, and its nearby harbor facilities at Beşiktepe, would have played host to the crews of these ships and their passengers, be they merchants, diplomats, or warriors.

The goods found by archaeologists in the ruins of Troy VI provide evidence of the city's wealth. Imported objects from Mesopotamia,

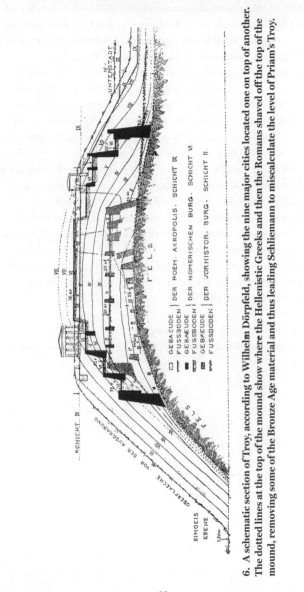

6. A schematic section of Troy, according to Wilhelm Dörpfeld, showing the nine major cities located one on top of another. The dotted lines at the top of the mound show where the Hellenistic Greeks and then the Romans shaved off the top of the mound, removing some of the Bronze Age material and thus leading Schliemann to miscalculate the level of Priam's Troy.

Egypt, and Cyprus were discovered during the careful excavations by Dörpfeld in the years after Schliemann's death, as well as by the later excavators, Carl Blegen and Manfred Korfmann. Mycenaean pottery was also found by all of the excavators, including Schliemann and especially Dörpfeld. Finding such Mycenaean objects in Troy VI may seem strange, in light of the possible ten-year siege of the city by Agamemnon and his warriors, until one remembers that, even according to Homer, the Mycenaeans and the Trojans were trading partners and friendly before the war.

Dörpfeld found that Troy VI, after going through a series of phases, was ultimately destroyed after hundreds of years of continuous inhabitation. He believed that the Mycenaeans had captured the city, burning it to the ground, and that it was this event that formed the basis of Homer's epic tales. This discovery, he believed, would end the debate. In his book *Troja und Ilion*, published in 1902, Dörpfeld wrote that "The long dispute over the existence of Troy and over its site is at an end. The Trojans have triumphed . . . Schliemann has been vindicated."

Contrary to Dörpfeld's belief, however, it may not have been humans who caused the destruction of Troy VI, but rather Mother Nature.

Chapter 6
Returning to Hisarlik: Carl Blegen and Manfred Korfmann

Carl Blegen began his excavations at Hisarlik on behalf of the University of Cincinnati in 1932, three decades after Dörpfeld published his words about "the end of the long dispute." Nobody had dug at the mound in the interim. Such a gap is not unusual at prominent sites, regardless of where they are in the world, for sustained excavations take a tremendous degree of commitment, funding, and preparation. There are also often months or years of negotiations involved, in order to procure the necessary permits from the proper authorities, who do not grant such permissions readily, especially if the site is deemed particularly significant.

Blegen disagreed with Dörpfeld's identification of Troy VI as Priam's Troy. He believed there was indisputable evidence that the final phase of Troy VI had been destroyed not by humans but by Mother Nature—specifically an earthquake. Instead of Troy VI, Blegen favored the next city, Troy VIIa, as Priam's Troy.

Blegen published a semi-popular book, *Troy and the Trojans* (1963), in which he described the situation at the site as his excavation team found it when they began reinvestigating the Troy VI phases. Despite the fact that the entire top of the mound had been shaved off during Hellenistic and Roman times as part of the construction for the Temple of Athena, and that what little survived was later removed by Schliemann, along the edges they found undisturbed deposits still remaining, 15 to 18 feet (5–6 m) deep, just inside the fortification wall. Within this "massive accumulation," as he called it, were the eight successive strata from Troy VIa to VIh (see fig. 7).

Blegen found that the eight layers contained the entire history of Troy VI without a cultural break, meaning that the inhabitants had simply been reorganizing and remodeling their city during the course of centuries without foreign interruption. Although the pottery changed over time, as did the architecture, overall it was clear that generation after generation of Trojans had lived in this city. There were some minor destructions and disturbances,

7. A plan of Troy I–IX, showing the different levels of the cities buried in the ancient mound of Hisarlik, with Troy VI expanded for a better view.

such as in phase VIf, dated to the late fifteenth or early fourteenth century BCE, when the remains of a fire were detected, but on the whole there was cultural continuity for the entire period of Troy VI, meaning no massive incursions of new residents or invaders.

Even the next phase in the site's history, known to archaeologists as Troy VIIa, showed similar cultural continuity with the previous city. In fact, both Dörpfeld and Blegen agreed that it was not really a new city—it was simply Troy VIh rebuilt, with the walls patched up and the houses restored. Even while Blegen was digging at the site from 1932 to 1938, Dörpfeld suggested (in 1935) that Troy VIIa should really be called Troy VIi, the ninth phase to this city, rather than the first phase of a new city. However, as Blegen stated, while this would "certainly correspond with the observed facts . . . we have kept the established terminology in order to avoid confusing those who have long been familiar with it." Manfred Korfmann, excavating again at the site fifty years after Blegen, made a similar comment: "It should be observed that even Dörpfeld had pointed out that, due to its close similarity to the preceding period, Phase VIIa really should be assigned to Period VI—that is, VIi. . . . On the basis of recent findings, we also prefer this classification."

Evidence for an earthquake

Blegen agreed with Dörpfeld in many instances, including that the site had been destroyed at the end of Troy VIh, for his excavations too yielded evidence of massive fire and destruction, although he disagreed as to how and why it had been destroyed. According to Blegen, there was no evidence of invaders, no new types of pottery, no major changes that might indicate the city had been destroyed by the Mycenaeans or anyone else.

There is even Mycenaean pottery found in Troy VIIa, much of it local imitations made by either Trojans or resident Mycenaeans, which would make no sense if the Mycenaeans had completely destroyed the city at the end of Troy VI and left it a smoking ruin, as Homer describes. Instead, it looks as if the Mycenaeans were still trading with the Trojans, or at least were still in contact with them during much of the time of Troy VIIa, which lasted for more than a century. All of this indicated to Blegen that the inhabitants—the survivors of whatever had destroyed the final city of Troy VI—had simply rebuilt the city and carried on, initiating the next phase of this long-lived sixth city, which had already been built and rebuilt in a series of different phases for more than four hundred years.

Thus, while Dörpfeld believed that the Mycenaeans had captured Troy VIh, burning it to the ground, and that it was this event that formed the basis of Homer's epic tales, Blegen, noting the continuity between Troy VIh and Troy VIIa, respectfully disagreed. He felt that Troy VIh had been destroyed by an earthquake, not by humans. If so, this would not have been the first time, for there is also evidence for earthquake damage in earlier cities—Troy III, IV, and V—and it is known that the site of Hisarlik is situated near the great North Anatolian fault line, which is still seismically active today, as shown by earthquakes that devastated the region in the late 1990s.

Blegen's evidence supporting his hypothesis that Troy VIh was destroyed by an earthquake is substantial—walls knocked out of kilter, huge towers collapsed, and everywhere the signs of tremendous force and upheaval (see fig. 8). As he noted in the final report published by the excavation team, "we feel confident in attributing the disaster to a severe earthquake. . . . A violent earthquake shock will account more convincingly than any probable human agency for the toppling of the city wall." A later re-examination by a respected geoarchaeologist agreed with Blegen's conclusion, stating, "the evidence supplied by the Cincinnati excavators . . . seems overwhelming."

Some scholars have argued that the Mycenaeans could have taken advantage of this earthquake that hit Troy, and that they may have

8. Collapsed stones and damaged walls indicate possible earthquake damage, in a photo taken during the excavations of Troy VI by Carl Blegen in the 1930s.

entered through the suddenly ruined walls which had fortuitously and dramatically been brought tumbling down. This in turn leads to an identification problem, for while Troy VI fits with Homer's description in many ways—its walls are big enough, its houses are grand enough, its streets are broad enough, it is wealthy enough—Homer makes no mention of an earthquake.

Enter the Trojan Horse. Although a number of scholars have suggested that the Trojan Horse was actually a battering ram or some other machine of war, the German academician Fritz Schachermeyr has proposed that the Trojan Horse was not a machine of war but was instead a poetic metaphor for an earthquake. His reasoning is simple: Poseidon was the Greek god of earthquakes; and Poseidon was usually represented by a horse (just as Athena was represented by an owl). The pounding of the horses' hooves, while pulling Poseidon in his chariot, not only created the crashing sound of the ocean's waves, according to the ancient Greeks, but also the sound that accompanies an earthquake. Therefore, the Trojan Horse may be Homer's way of depicting the earthquake sent by Poseidon to level the walls of Troy. The Trojan Horse is, quite literally, the earthquake, but only metaphorically speaking. This is an ingenious suggestion but is perhaps a bit farfetched. But if we put ourselves into Homer's position, it is one of the only ways to end the story without actually changing the real historical ending of the city. Besides, there is no other way, if one wants Troy VI to be Priam's Troy, to explain why the city fits Homer's description in every way except for the manner of its destruction.

Redating and reuse

A recent re-examination of the imported and local Mycenaean pottery found in the Troy VIh levels has redated the destruction of this city. Blegen had originally dated this pottery to ca. 1275 BCE, but later scholars argued about this date, with some even suggesting that it could be as late as 1130–1100 BCE. The new study was done in the 1990s by Penelope Mountjoy, a well-respected scholar and author of several authoritative volumes on Mycenaean pottery, who was able to handle and re-examine all of the sherds found by Blegen for the first time in many decades. In her detailed paper she concluded that Troy VIh was destroyed most likely ca. 1300 BCE. She also agreed with Blegen that it was probably ended by an earthquake, which had nothing to do with Agamemnon or the Mycenaeans.

Blegen noticed that the ruins of the large and prosperous houses located within the citadel of Troy VIh were either immediately rebuilt and reused in Troy VIIa, but now with many party walls subdividing their interiors, as if many families were living where a single family unit had lived previously, or else had ramshackle huts and houses built over their remains, using the stubs of the walls from the ruined fine houses. He also noticed other indications that he thought meant that the population of this fortified citadel had suddenly expanded to many times its previous size. A prime indication of this population explosion, to his mind, was the many storage jars—*pithoi* as they are known—not only within the houses but also buried beneath the floors so that only their tops were visible and accessible. By burying these jars, the inhabitants were able to keep some perishable items cold, even in an era that had no refrigeration, and they were also able to double or even triple their overall storage capacity for grain, wine, olive oil, and other necessities of life.

Destruction of Troy VIIa

Blegen was certain that he was excavating a city that had been besieged, and that the population from the lower city and perhaps from the surrounding villages had flooded the wealthy upper citadel of the town in the face of an advancing enemy force. His suspicions were confirmed, he believed, by the discovery that Troy VIIa had been destroyed by warfare, for he found skeletons, or portions of unburied bodies, in the streets within the citadel, as well as arrowheads, of specifically Aegean manufacture, and evidence of fire and of houses destroyed by burning. He and his fellow excavators wrote in their final report that the remains of Troy VIIa were "everywhere marked by the ravages of fire," adding that the "scattered remnants of human bones discovered in the fire-scarred ruins of Settlement VIIA surely indicate that its destruction was accompanied by violence (see fig. 9). Little imagination is required to see reflected here the fate of an ancient town captured and sacked by implacable foes."

Clearly, Blegen said, it was Troy VIIa, not Troy VIh, which had been put to the torch by the Mycenaeans. He dated this destruction to ca. 1260–1240 BCE, based on his dating of the pottery and perhaps on his desire to link this stratum to the Trojan War. He knew that if the Mycenaeans were involved in the Trojan War, as described by Homer, they would have had to participate before their own civilization was under attack and their own palaces on the Greek mainland were being destroyed—in some places, this began about 1225 BCE. In his 1963 book, *Troy and the Trojans*,

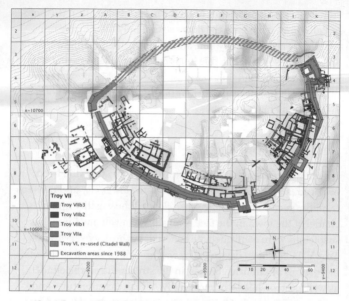

9. A plan of Troy VIIa, with the reused wall of Troy VI indicated, from the excavations at the site led by Manfred Korfmann from 1988 to 2005.

Blegen concluded: "The fire-blackened wreckage and ruins of the settlement offer a vivid picture of the harsh fate that was regularly meted out to a town besieged, captured and looted by implacable enemies, as is so graphically described in the accounts of marauding expeditions in the Homeric poems."

Having ascertained to his satisfaction that Troy VIIA was Priam's Troy, Blegen pointed also to the next city, constructed directly upon the ashes and burned debris, that previous excavators had already labeled Troy VIIb. Blegen was able to subdivide it into two separate phases, VIIb₁ and VIIb₂. The first of these two subphases, VIIb₁, showed great similarities to Troy VIIa, and Blegen therefore concluded that it was evidence for "an immediate reoccupation of the site by the survivors who somehow escaped the disaster that laid the citadel of Troy VIIa in smoldering ruins." At one point, in fact, he wrote again, "had we felt ourselves entirely free to modify Dörpfeld's numbering of the layers on the site, we should more properly have recognized the cultural connections of Troy VIIa and VIIb$_1$ by renaming them respectively Troy VIi and Troy VIj." The subphase lasted about a generation, according to Blegen, but he was not clear what caused it to come to an end ca. 1150 BCE, for he could detect no signs of violence, no burning, no looting, no sacking of the VIIb$_1$ city. He simply called it an unsolved mystery and left it at that.

The second of the two subphases, Troy VIIb$_2$, was completely different from everything that had come before. Had he been able to do so, Blegen would rather have called it Troy VIII because it was so different. Troy VIIb$_2$ was not simply the second phase of the same city; now the town plan was completely altered, the architecture of the houses unlike what had come before, and the pottery new and different. The inhabitants of Troy VIIb$_2$ were obviously different; it was as if the previous occupants of Troy VIIb$_1$ had totally vanished. This subphase, in turn, lasted for two or three generations before the site was again destroyed, perhaps by enemy action or another earthquake ca. 1100 BCE. Troy was then abandoned for several centuries, eventually to be re-inhabited later, starting in the Iron Age ca. 700 BCE and then continuing through the Roman period and beyond.

Problems with Blegen's interpretation

So had Blegen finally solved the mystery and identified the city of the Trojan War? Was it really Troy VIIa? There are several problems with his identification. For one thing, Troy VIIa does not fit Homer's description of a wealthy city—a city with towering gates, high walls, broad streets, large houses, and a magnificent palace. The city that Blegen excavated was a poor city, a reconstructed city, with its large houses subdivided by party walls and with storage jars buried underfoot. Blegen thought that it was a city under siege; Penelope Mountjoy has more recently suggested that it was simply a city trying to recover initially from a devastating earthquake, complete with temporary houses hastily erected amongst the ruins. Regardless, it was not a city that would have taken ten years to capture, and it certainly was not a city worth writing an epic about. In fact, the only way Troy VIIa matches Homer's story is in the manner in which it was destroyed—in a deliberate act of war. Perhaps Homer was writing about the magnificent city of Troy VI but also about the destruction of Troy VIIa—in other words, taking a poet's liberty by telescoping events in order to create a grand epic tale. But this is only one possible scenario.

In addition, Blegen's dating of the destruction of Troy VIIa has been challenged several times in the past half century, always on the basis of the pottery found in the settlement, with some scholars dating the destruction as late as 1050 BCE. Most recently it has been redated by Mountjoy to the last decades of the thirteenth century BCE and the first decades of the twelfth century BCE, sometime between 1230 BCE and 1190/80 BCE, based upon her personal re-analysis of the pottery. This might make it difficult to argue that the Mycenaeans were responsible for this destruction, unless the Mycenaean palaces back on the Greek mainland were being attacked and destroyed precisely because all of their warriors were away fighting at Troy. In fact, Mountjoy suggests that Troy VIIa was not destroyed by the Mycenaeans, but rather by the Sea Peoples, and that the city which the Mycenaeans destroyed is the much-later Troy VIIb$_2$ city, ca. 1100 BCE, although this latter suggestion is far too late to be likely.

The timing is certainly right for the Sea Peoples to have attacked and destroyed Troy VIIa, as part of their larger campaign of destruction, and some have suggested that survivors of the ravaged city joined the Sea Peoples in their subsequent activities. It is, however, not clear whether the Sea Peoples ever actually attacked Troy, and so the identity of the destroyers of Troy VIIa remains an open question, as does the destruction of Troy VIIb$_1$ and VIIb$_2$.

Korfmann at Troy

Exactly fifty years after Blegen's excavations at Troy ended, the next set began, in 1988. They were led by Manfred Korfmann of the University of Tübingen in Germany, who was interested in investigating the Bronze Age levels at the site. In coordination with Korfmann, investigations of the post–Bronze Age levels at the site (the Hellenistic and Roman remains) were also resumed, directed first by Stella Miller of Bryn Mawr College and then by C. Brian Rose of the University of Cincinnati.

Korfmann and his Bronze Age team started with a thorough re-examination of the Early Bronze Age remains in the center of the mound and also collected radiocarbon samples from all periods, the first time this had been done at the site. Later, they were primarily concerned with re-investigating the cities of Troy VI and VII in order to determine how large the cities were, what life was like there during the Late Bronze Age, and what exactly happened to these cities that brought each of them to dramatic endings.

Korfmann steadfastly maintained that he was not investigating the Trojan War, nor was he even interested in either proving or disproving the legend, but rather that he was investigating a very interesting Late Bronze Age city, one that had international connections and was a powerhouse in the region during the end of the second millennium BCE. By 2001, however, Korfmann was convinced that the city that he was excavating, Troia, as he called it in German, could be conclusively identified with the city known to the Hittites as Wilusa. From then on, his excavation reports refer to the site as Troia/Wilusa, an identification accepted by many other scholars.

Korfmann and his team made many discoveries, through both excellent excavation techniques and high-tech equipment. For one thing, they found and identified one more subphase, Troy VIIb$_3$, which lasted nearly a century and ended for an unknown reason about 1000 BCE, just before the site was abandoned for several hundred years.

They also found the first piece of writing ever discovered at the site—a biconvex bronze seal, inscribed on either side. Found in level VIIb$_2$ in 1995 and dating to ca. 1100 BCE, the seal has a man's name on one side and a woman's name on the other, and an indication that the man may have been a scribe.

The lower city

By far the most important of their discoveries, and certainly the largest, was made soon after the commencement of the project in 1988. Within a few years, Korfmann and his team were certain that they had detected, through the use of remote sensing equipment, the existence of an enormous lower city, stretching for more than 1,300 feet (400 m) south of the actual

Table 2. Chronology of Hisarlik/Troy Strata, ca. 1300–1000 BCE

Site Level	Approximate End Date	Probable Cause of Destruction	Aftermath
Troy VIh	1300 BCE	Earthquake	Continuity/ rebuilding
Troy VIIa	1230–1190/80 BCE	Attacked by enemy	Continuity/ rebuilding
Troy VIIb$_1$	1150 BCE	Unknown	New Culture
Troy VIIb$_2$	1100 BCE	Earthquake or Attacked by enemy	Continuity/ rebuilding
Troy VIIb$_3$	1000 BCE	Unknown	Abandoned for centuries

mound of Hisarlik. This discovery increases both the size and the population of Troy ten to fifteen times beyond that which was previously suspected. It also makes it clear that Late Bronze Age Troy was indeed a wealthy and prosperous city, covering 50 to 75 acres (200–300,000 sq m) and probably housing between four thousand and ten thousand inhabitants. As the investigation continued for more than a dozen years, through 2005, the archaeologists were able to confirm that virtually all of the fields surrounding the mound of Hisarlik covered this entire lower city, including levels dating to Troy VI and VIIa, in addition to later ruins above them laid out in an established north–south/east–west grid, dating to the Hellenistic and Roman periods. In fact, the remains from the later periods completely covered those of the Bronze Age lower city, leaving them "ill-preserved" and "excavated only with difficulty and in small patches," in the words of one expedition member.

Korfmann's team used several different types of magnetometers, a category of remote sensing equipment that has become popular because it enables archaeologists to peer beneath the ground before beginning excavation. By measuring the strength of the local magnetic field within the intended excavation area at specific points, the team was able to create images of what lay below: the local magnetic field varies depending upon whether a wall lies below, or a ditch, or nothing at all. Actual excavation was then conducted to confirm the initial remote sensing findings.

It was now apparent that Schliemann, Dörpfeld, and Blegen had all been excavating just the citadel or upper part of the city where the palace lay, which measured only about 656 feet x 656 feet (200 m x 200 m). In retrospect, it is not surprising that there is a lower city at Troy, for most of the contemporary Mycenaean palatial sites have both a citadel and a lower city. But it took modern scientific equipment and some educated guesswork on the part of Korfmann and his team to find the lower city of Troy.

This technology, or at least its interpretation, is not infallible, though, and at one point Korfmann and his team were led astray. In February 1993, they announced to great fanfare that their remote sensing equipment had indicated the presence of something deep underground, which was encircling the lower city more than a thousand feet away from the citadel. The team interpreted their discovery as a tremendous fortification wall. This made headlines around the world. Upon excavation during that summer, however, it turned out that it was not a fortification wall at all but a large defensive ditch dating to the time of Troy VI, cut into bedrock and measuring between 3 and 6 feet (1–2 m) deep and up to 13 feet (4 m) wide. The ditch had filled up with dirt and garbage over the millennia and thus appeared on their scans as a solid mass, which they had initially misinterpreted as a wall.

In the first two years after its discovery (1993 and 1994), the team traced this ditch for more than a thousand feet. They later discovered that there was a 30-foot-wide (10 m) gate present. They also discovered that there were two such ditches, one placed farther out from the citadel and in use later than the other, apparently as the population expanded outward during the later part of Troy VI. There may also have been a wooden palisade, or high fence, originally placed behind each ditch, but which has long since disintegrated. The archaeologists were also able to trace the remains of the massive Troy VI stone wall surrounding the citadel, first found by Dörpfeld, exposing more than had been found by the previous excavators.

Between 1997 and 2001, Korfmann's team also completely excavated the so-called Spring Cave—interconnected man-made tunnels, shafts, and galleries comprising a water system carved into the living rock. This lay outside the walls of the citadel, in the southwestern section of the lower city. The main tunnel had been discovered early on during the renewed excavations, but it was thought to date to the Roman period, because of the remains of fish ponds and other constructions in and near the entrance to the tunnel. These remains in front do indeed date to the Roman period, but by 2001 Korfmann and his team were able to date the construction of the tunnel system back to the Early Bronze Age, during the third millennium BCE, and to show that it had been in use for the better part of two thousand years. This was extremely important for Korfmann, especially in terms of connecting Hisarlik/Troy with the city of Wilusa known from Hittite records, for this may be the "underground watercourse of the land of Wilusa" mentioned in the Alaksandu Treaty.

Korfmann and Troy VIIa

Korfmann, as had Blegen and Dörpfeld before him, took pains to make clear that there was no cultural break between Troy VIh and Troy VIIa. Where Korfmann departed from his predecessors was in seeing Troy VIIa (or VIi) as having lasted for more than a century. Citing Penelope Mountjoy and her re-examination of the Mycenaean pottery, Korfmann declared that Troy VIIa begins about 1300 BCE and ends, after several building phases, ca. 1180 BCE "due to destruction caused by war."

Among the most dramatic of Korfmann's discoveries, as early as 1995, was evidence in the lower city that the Troy VIIa period had come to an end in fire and war. As he noted in a preliminary report, their excavations revealed a burned layer southwest of the citadel mound, dating to the end of Troia VIIa, which they believed was the result of "a military event." Later, in the popular magazine *Archaeology*, he noted that they had found some skeletons and "heaps of sling bullets" in this area, which eventually was shown to contain the remains of a large Courtyard House with storerooms. Interestingly, directly underneath this Troy VIIa Courtyard House is a building from phase Troy VIh, which was also completely burned and destroyed as the result of an earthquake, in Korfmann's opinion. Thus, in a single small area, Korfmann had found evidence for a Troy VIIa building destroyed by enemy action overlying a Troy VIh building destroyed by an earthquake.

Over the years, Korfmann's team discovered in the lower city bronze arrowheads, at least one skeleton from an unburied body of a young girl, and several piles of what may be sling stones ready to be used by the defenders (see fig. 10). One of his team members described the situation as indicative of a lost war and indeed, for Korfmann at least, all of this was clear evidence of a city under attack by enemy forces. At one point, in a BBC documentary broadcast in 2004, he reported: "Now the evidence is burning and catastrophe with fire. Then there are skeletons; we found, for example, a girl, I think sixteen, seventeen years old, half buried, the feet were burned by fire. Half of the corpse was underground. This is strange [that] a rapid burial was in [a] public space,

10. Arrowheads recovered from the Troy VIIa stratum in the lower city at Troy indicate that the city was destroyed in battle by a hostile force.

inside the city . . . and we found sling pellets in heaps. . . . It was a city which was besieged. It was a city which was defended, which protected itself. They lost the war and obviously they were defeated." However, Korfmann does not specify by whom he thinks the destruction was caused, nor does he comment on the fact that the Mycenaean civilization was in an advanced stage of disruption at that time.

In fact, it is not at all clear who caused the destruction of the lower city. Such bronze arrowheads could have been used by the Mycenaeans, but they could also have been used by the Sea Peoples or someone else entirely. If the event that caused the destruction of the city were to be dated as late as 1180 BCE, as Korfmann indicated, then the destruction could as readily be linked with the second invasion of the Sea Peoples during the time of Ramses III as it could with the Mycenaeans. This dating, though, is based on the latest possible date for the Mycenaean pottery analyzed by Mountjoy, so the attack could just as easily have taken place a few decades earlier, according to the same study. If that were the case, then the destruction could be linked to the initial overthrow of Walmu, king of Wilusa, as recorded in the Hittite tablets, and could implicate the Mycenaeans after all. This hypothesis, however, is highly speculative.

A new Trojan War

Although it is still not clear whether Troy VIIa was destroyed by the Mycenaeans or by someone else, Korfmann's new findings may eventually lead to an answer for the question of the Trojan War. His data, like those of most archaeologists, are nonetheless subject to interpretation. In this regard, Korfmann's work has already come under attack from a surprising quarter—one of his own colleagues at the University of Tübingen, Frank Kolb.

Beginning in the summer of 2001, during a large exhibit on Troy that opened in Stuttgart, then went to Braunschweig and finally to Bonn, Kolb accused Korfmann of exaggeration, misleading statements, and shoddy scholarship in connection with his excavations at Troy. Kolb claimed that there was no lower city at Troy and that both the lower city and the ditch hewn in the bedrock were figments of Korfmann's imagination, intended to deceive the general public.

The discussions grew in intensity and ultimately led to a two-day conference—almost a mock trial—at the university in February 2002. It was attended by more than eight hundred people per day. A three-hour general discussion during the second day was broadcast live on radio to a riveted audience throughout much of Germany. More than sixty journalists covered the proceedings. According to one reporter, the conference ended in a fistfight between Korfmann and Kolb, "an unseemly bout of fisticuffs," as the journalist called it, but the eventual ruling was in favor of Korfmann and his interpretation of Troy, supported soon thereafter by a long reassessment penned by some of the Bronze Age specialists who had been at the conference. Kolb did not give up the battle, however, and the debate has continued in the pages of academic journals.

Korfmann died suddenly in August 2005. With his death, Korfmann's banner has been taken up by his colleagues at Troy, Tübingen, Sheffield, and elsewhere. The Bronze Age excavations at Troy conducted by the University of Tübingen have continued, first during the summer of 2005 in the capable hands of Korfmann's deputy, Peter Jablonka, and since then under the leadership of Korfmann's senior colleague, Ernst Pernicka.

Epilogue

In the end, what do we know and what do we believe about the Trojan War? Was Homer describing a real historical event that took place toward the end of the Late Bronze Age, perhaps the final conflict fought by the Mycenaeans on the coast of Anatolia before their own civilization collapsed? Much has been written about Troy and the Trojan War in both the distant and the recent past. Assertions that Troy was located in England, Scandinavia, or even Cilicia in Turkey, that the story was actually a garbled version of the legend of Atlantis, and other flights of fantasy have found their way into print, some even in recent years. Scholars themselves are still arguing about the historicity of Homer and the Trojan War, with some saying that the Homeric poems should be regarded as mere fantasies but others stating that it is inconceivable that "the Trojan War motif . . . could have been invented out of nothing in the eighth century."

Two questions remain paramount. Was there an actual war fought in northwestern Anatolia on which Homer's *Iliad* was based? Have we excavated the site where Priam's Troy once stood? Naysayers aside, most scholars would agree that the answer to both questions is yes, but a qualified yes. The problem in providing a definitive answer is not that we have too little data but that we have too much. The Greek epics, Hittite records, Luwian poetry, and archaeological remains provide evidence not of a single Trojan war but rather of multiple wars, which were fought in the area that we identify as Troy and the Troad. As a result, the evidence for the Trojan War of Homer is tantalizing but equivocal. There is no single "smoking gun."

How many wars?

According to the Greek literary evidence, there were at least two Trojan Wars (Heracles's and Agamemnon's), not simply one; in fact, there were three wars, if one counts Agamemnon's earlier abortive attack on Teuthrania. Similarly, according to the Hittite literary evidence, there were at least four Trojan Wars, ranging from the Assuwa Rebellion in the late fifteenth century BCE to the overthrow of Walmu, king of Wilusa in the late thirteenth century BCE. And, according to the archaeological evidence, Troy/Hisarlik was destroyed twice, if not three times, between 1300 and 1000 BCE. Some of this has long been known; the rest has come to light more recently.

Unfortunately, none of these individual events can be correlated to another with certainty. For instance, one would think that the overthrow of Walmu, seen in the relevant Hittite records, would be reflected in the destruction of Troy VIIa, but we cannot say with complete confidence that the two are definitely linked.

This, though, is a common problem in archaeology of these early periods—even when one has destructions attested archaeologically at a site on the one hand and written records documenting the capture and/or destruction of the same city on the other, it is frequently difficult to link the two. The best example that comes to mind is that of Megiddo in Israel, where we know, from written records, that the Egyptian pharaoh Thutmose III captured the city in about 1479 BCE. We also have several archaeological strata at the site that indicate destructions. However, it has proved impossible so far to correlate the written texts and the archaeological evidence.

It also must be made clear that any attempt to locate the Trojan War historically and archaeologically is still necessarily based on a circumstantial case, which invokes a series of assumptions and observations, resulting in a plausible but still hypothetical reconstruction. These include the following, some or all of which can be used:

- Wilusa is probably (W)ilios (Troy).
- Alaksandu, king of Wilusa, may be Alexander/ Paris of (W)ilios/Troy.
- Walmu, king of Wilusa, is deposed by enemy forces in the late thirteenth century BCE.
- Ahhiyawa probably is/are the Mycenaeans from mainland Greece.
- Troy VIh was destroyed but probably by an earthquake rather than by humans.
- Troy VIIa was destroyed by humans, in warfare.

Homer and history

One may argue that it is quite conceivable that Homer used literary license to telescope people and events, and several centuries of intermittent warfare, in order to create a compelling epic poem centered around a ten-year struggle. His poem was not meant to be a history book but rather an epic of national pride concerned with universal themes such as love and honor.

Among the material that Homer might have drawn upon, in addition to his understanding of the Bronze Age Aegean world of warriors and weapons, would have been tales of the Assuwa Rebellion, and probable Mycenaean involvement therein, in the time of Tudhaliya I/II ca. 1420 BCE, as well as knowledge of the wealthy city of Troy VIh, destroyed by an earthquake ca. 1300 BCE. The oral traditions might also have told of the rebuilt city of Troy VIIa, ruled over first by Alaksandu ca. 1280 BCE in the time of Muwatalli II and then by Walmu ca. 1225 or later in the time of Tudhaliya IV, as well as perhaps the animosity between the Hittites and Ahhiyawa over Wilusa in the time of Hattusili III in the middle of the thirteenth century BCE. He would also probably have heard of the destruction of Troy VIIa in warfare ca. 1230–1180 BCE, and perhaps even the later destruction of Troy VIIb$_2$ ca. 1100 BCE.

Thus, Homer's descriptions of Troy in the *Iliad* could be drawn from knowledge of Troy VIh, while the description of its destruction could be drawn from awareness of the fires that brought an end to Troy VIIa. If so, one could argue that Homer's Trojan War was a process rather than an event, incorporating details of people, places, and events taken from several hundred years during the Late Bronze Age, not to mention the subsequent five hundred years that lay between the war and Homer himself. Homer could have woven material from older epics into that of his own, incorporating boars'-tusk helmets, tower shields, and earlier figures such as Ajax, as well as updating the equipment and tactics used in some cases—to better fit his own time—and used descriptions of the lovely and forbidding city of Troy VI in place of Walmu's more ramshackle and rebuilt Troy VIIa.

Homer may not have had his facts straight, nor might he have cared. After all, some of the greatest epic poets and poetry since medieval times have altered the facts of history as we know them and sometimes a great heroic tradition is built around an event, which was of minor significance or which has been so distorted that it is no longer recognizable; one need only point to the *Chanson de Roland* and the *Niebelungleid*, both of which altered the details of actual historical events. Perhaps we should be content, therefore, with the knowledge that the basic parameters of the tale of the Trojan War can be confirmed, even if some of the details can be questioned, for we have come much farther than some might realize.

Since the days of Schliemann, we have confirmed the existence of the Mycenaeans and their civilization, even if we have not yet shown that Agamemnon once existed. We have confirmed that the city of Troy did once exist, even if we have not yet shown conclusively which level at the site belonged to Priam, or even if he too ever actually existed. We have confirmed, or at least can surmise with a great deal of confidence, that Mycenaean warriors were fighting on the coast of northwestern Anatolia, in the precise region of Troy, on and off again over the course of more than three centuries during the Late Bronze Age, even if we cannot point specifically to Achilles and Patroclus. And, we now know that Hittite records indicate numerous wars or conflicts fought at or over Troy during that same time period, even if we cannot definitively say that it was Agamemnon who fought Alaksandu in the early thirteenth century BCE or deposed Walmu in the late thirteenth century BCE. In other words, the basic outline of Homer's story rings true, whether or not Alexander and Helen, Agamemnon and Priam, or Achilles and Hector actually existed.

But would the Trojan War have been fought because of love for a woman? Could a ten-year war have been instigated by the kidnapping of a single person? The answer, of course, is yes, just as an Egypto-Hittite war in the thirteenth century BCE was touched off by the death of a Hittite prince, and the outbreak of World War I was sparked by the assassination of Archduke Ferdinand. But just as one could argue that World War I would have taken place anyway, perhaps triggered by some other event, so one can argue that the Trojan War would inevitably have taken place, with or without Helen. The presumptive kidnapping of Helen can be seen merely an excuse to launch a preordained war for control of land, trade, profit, and access to the Black Sea.

Would such a war have lasted for ten years? That seems unlikely, of course, and it may be that there are other factors in play here. Perhaps there was a nine-year gap between the initial raid on Teuthrania and the final attack on Troy, as some have suggested. Perhaps it is as Barry Strauss, a classics professor at Cornell University, has suggested, that the ten years simply reflect a Near Eastern expression, "nine times and then a tenth," meaning simply a very long time. Or perhaps it really did last ten years. We may never know.

In addition, it may be that the real basis for the Trojan War had nothing to do with the Trojans themselves. Troy lay on the edge of both the Mycenaean Empire and the Hittite Empire, in what one might call a "contested periphery," and was caught in between two of the great powers in the ancient Mediterranean world. Both sides thought that they should possess Troy, and both sides were willing to go to war for control of the city. What the Trojans themselves wanted would have been irrelevant, or at least of little consequence. Thus, we have the distinct possibility that the Trojan War was actually fought between the Mycenaeans and the Hittites, with the Trojans being the hapless peoples caught in the middle (but whom both Homer and the Hittite records saw as being on the side of the Hittites, against the Mycenaeans/Ahhiyawa).

A war for the ages

And, of course, artistic and literary reinterpretations of the Trojan War and the fate of its better-known participants, including Odysseus, have been produced and reproduced over the centuries, up to and including the present. Thus, we have not only the later Greek playwrights and the Roman poets but also Chaucer's *Troilus and Criseyde*, Shakespeare's *Troilus and Cressida*, Camille

Saint-Saëns's opera *Hélène* (1904), James Joyce's *Ulysses*, and the silver screen's various takes on the epic, with numerous films appearing since the early twentieth century featuring the Trojan War, Helen, Achilles, Odysseus, and/or the Trojan Horse.

Some of these later works contain parts that may be considered inaccurate or unfaithful to Homer in details or plot—the 2004 Hollywood blockbuster movie, for instance, has no gods or goddesses in sight; Brad Pitt anachronistically placing coins on the closed eyes of dead Patroclus five hundred years before such currency is invented in Lydia ca. 700 BCE; and both Agamemnon and Menelaus killed at Troy while Paris/Alexander is not, thereby changing the familiar Homeric/*Epic Cycle* version—but this is a long-standing tradition going back to the Greek playwrights who followed Homer and who also felt free to change some of the details. More importantly, each has reinterpreted the story in its own way, with changes and nuances frequently reflecting the angst and desires of that particular age, such as medieval Christianity for Chaucer, the Elizabethan worldview for Shakespeare, and the Iraq war for *Troy* director Wolfgang Peterson.

The relevance to wars of all ages is obvious, and is perhaps most exemplified by an untitled poem by Patrick Shaw-Stewart, a classics scholar from Oxford who fought at Gallipoli in World War I, just across the Dardanelles from Troy. He wrote in part:

> O hell of ships and cities,
> Hell of men like me,
> Fatal second Helen,
> Why must I follow thee?
>
> Achilles came to Troyland
> And I to Chersonese;
> He turned from wrath to battle,
> And I from three days' peace.

Was it so hard, Achilles,
So very hard to die?
Thou knewest, and I know not—
So much the happier I.

In 1964, the eminent historian Moses Finley suggested that we should move the narrative of the Trojan War from the realm of history into the realm of myth and poetry until we have more evidence. Many would argue that we now have that additional evidence, particularly in the form of the Hittite texts discussing Ahhiyawa and Wilusa and the new archaeological data from Troy. However, we have seen that there was no specific "Trojan War" that one can definitively point to, at least not as Homer has described it in the *Iliad* and the *Odyssey*. Instead, we have found several such Trojan wars and several cities at Troy, enough that one can conclude there is a historical kernel of truth—of some sort—underlying all the stories.

The lines between reality and fantasy might be blurred, particularly when Zeus, Hera, and other gods become involved in the war, and we might quibble about some of the details, but overall, Troy and the Trojan War are right where they should be, in northwestern Anatolia and firmly ensconced in the world of the Late Bronze Age, as we now know from archaeology and Hittite records, in addition to the Greek literary evidence from both Homer and the *Epic Cycle*. Moreover, the enduring themes of love, honor, war, kinship, and obligations, which so resonated with the later Greeks and then the Romans, have continued to reverberate through the ages from Aeschylus, Sophocles, and Euripides to Virgil, Ovid, and Livy, and thence to Chaucer, Shakespeare, and beyond, so that the story still holds broad appeal even today, more than three thousand years after the original events, or some variation thereof, took place.

Glossary: characters and places

Achilles: Greek hero
Aeschylus: Greek playwright; lived in the fifth century BCE
Aethiopis: part of the Epic Cycle
Agamemnon: brother of Menelaus; king of Mycenae on mainland Greece
Agias of Troezen: probable author of the *Returns*
Ahhiyawa: probable Hittite name for Mycenaean Greece
Ajax: Greek hero; possibly from even earlier Greek myths
Akkadian: language spoken and written in the second millennium BCE ancient Near East; the diplomatic *lingua franca* of the time
Alaksandu: king of Wilusa; ruled ca. 1280 BCE
Alaksandu Treaty: lengthy treaty signed between Alaksandu of Wilusa and the Hittite king Muwattalli II, ca. 1280 BCE
Alexander: alternate name for Paris, prince of Troy; son of Priam; lover of Helen
Aphrodite: Greek goddess of love and beauty
Arctinus of Miletus: probable author of the *Aethiopis* and the *Sack of Troy*
Arnuwanda I: Hittite king, successor of Tudhaliya I/II; ruled ca. 1420 BCE
Assuwa: confederacy of twenty-two city-states in western Anatolia ca. 1420 BCE
Athena: Greek goddess of wisdom, courage, and other attributes
Attarissiya: a ruler of Ahhiya (Ahhiyawa)
Clytemnestra: wife of Agamemnon
Cypria: part of the Epic Cycle

Cyprias of Halicarnassus: possible author of the *Cypria*

Epeius: Greek warrior who had the idea for the Trojan Horse

Epic Cycle: fragmentary collection of epic tales about the Trojan War

Euripides: Greek playwright; lived in the fifth century BCE

Hattusili III: Hittite king; ruled ca. 1267–1237 BCE

Hector: Trojan hero

Hecuba: wife of King Priam of Troy

Hegesias of Salamis: possible author of the *Cypria*

Helen: wife of Menelaus; queen of Mycenaean Sparta; lover of Alexander/Paris

Hera: wife of Zeus

Heracles: Greek hero; attacked Troy in the generation before the Trojan War

Herodotus: Greek historian; lived in the fifth century BCE

Hisarlik: mound most likely containing the ancient site of Troy

Hittite: language spoken and written in second millennium BCE Anatolia (Turkey)

Hittites: major power in Anatolia (modern Turkey), ca. 1700–1200 BCE

Homer: purported author of the *Iliad* and the *Odyssey*; lived ca. 750 BCE

Iliad: Homer's epic of the final days of the Trojan War

Ilios: alternate name for Troy; originally spelled (W)ilios

Iliupersis (Sack of Troy): part of the Epic Cycle

Iphigenia: daughter of Agamemnon; sacrificed at Aulis to ensure favorable winds for the Mycenaean fleet

Kukkulli: king of Assuwa, son of Piyama-Kurunta, ruled ca. 1420 BCE

Laomedon: king of Troy at the time of Heracles's attack; predecessor of Priam

Lesches of Mitylene: probable author of the *Little Iliad*

Little Iliad: part of the Epic Cycle

Luwian: language spoken and written in second millennium BCE Anatolia (Turkey)

Madduwatta: Hittite vassal who features prominently in the Ahhiyawa correspondence

Manapa-Tarhunta: king of the Seha River Land, south of the Troad; ruled in the thirteenth century BCE

Menelaus: husband of Helen; brother of Agamemnon; king of Mycenaean Sparta

Milawata: Hittite name for the city of Miletus, on the coast of Asia Minor/Anatolia

Milawata Letter: letter probably written and sent in the late thirteenth century BCE by the Hittite king Tudhaliya IV (ruled ca. 1237–1209 BCE); concerned with the city of Milawata (Miletus) as well as with the continuing activities of Piyamaradu, a "renegade Hittite" involved with Ahhiyawa.

Minoans: inhabitants of Bronze Age Crete, in the Aegean

Muwattalli II: Hittite king; ruled ca. 1295–1272 BCE

Mycenae: major city of the Mycenaeans, in the Peloponnesus region of the Greek mainland; inhabited ca. 1700–1100 BCE; first excavated by Schliemann in the 1870s

Mycenaeans: Achaeans; inhabitants of the Greek mainland from 1700–1200 BCE

Nestor: king of Pylos on the Greek mainland

Odysseus: Greek hero

Odyssey: Homer's epic of Odysseus's journey home after the Trojan War

Ovid: Roman poet; first century BCE to first century CE

Paris: alternate name for Alexander, prince of Troy; son of Priam; lover of Helen

Patroclus: faithful friend of Achilles; dies while fighting wearing Achilles's armor

Philoctetes: kills Achilles by shooting him in the heel with an arrow

Piyama-Kurunta: leader of the Assuwan Confederacy, prior to ca. 1420 BCE

Piyamaradu: a "renegade Hittite" who was involved with the Ahhiyawans in the thirteenth century BCE

Priam: king of Troy at the time of the Trojan War

Proclus: editor of the *Epic Cycle*, (i.e., the *Chrestomatheia Grammatiki*); lived in either the second or fifth century CE

Quintus Smyrnaeus: epic poet of the fifth century CE

Returns: part of the Epic Cycle

Sea Peoples: roving/migrating groups that came through the Mediterranean region twice, in 1207 and 1177 BCE; may have contributed to the end of the Late Bronze Age in the region

Sophocles: Greek playwright; lived in the fifth century BCE

Stasinus of Cyprus: possible author of the *Cypria*

Suppiluliuma I: one of the greatest Hittite kings; ruled ca. 1350–1322 BCE

Tawagalawa: brother of king of Ahhiyawa, mid-thirteenth century BCE; named in Hittite letter

Tawagalawa Letter: written by a king of Hatti, probably Hattusili III (ruled ca. 1267–1237 BCE), the letter is concerned with the activities of Piyamaradu, a "renegade Hittite," who was actively involved with Ahhiyawa (probably the Mycenaeans)

Telemachus: son of Odysseus

Teuthrania: area south of Troy, which Achilles and other Mycenaeans mistakenly attacked

Trojans: inhabitants of ancient Troy

Troy: Ilios; home to Priam, Alexander/Paris, and Hector; site of the Trojan War; probably to be identified with the site of Hisarlik in modern Turkey

Tudhaliya I/II: Hittite king who ruled ca. 1450–1420 and put down the Assuwa Rebellion

Tudhaliya IV: Hittite king; ruled ca. 1237–1209 BCE

Virgil: Roman epic poet; first century BCE

Walmu: king of Wilusa, late thirteenth century BCE

Wilusa: probable Hittite name for Troy (Ilios)

Zannanza: Hittite prince, son of Suppiluliuma I; killed enroute to Egypt in mid-fourteenth century BCE

Zeus: head of the pantheon of gods worshipped by the ancient Greeks

References

Throughout, translations from the *Iliad* follow A. T. Murray, *The Iliad, Books 1–12*; revised by William F. Wyatt (Cambridge, MA: Harvard University Press, 1999); Richmond Lattimore, *The Iliad of Homer* (Chicago: University of Chicago Press, 1961); or Robert Fagles, *Homer: The Iliad* (New York, Penguin, 1991). Those from the *Odyssey* follow A. T. Murray, *The Odyssey* (Cambridge, MA: Harvard University Press, 1984); from the *Epic Cycle* follow H. G. Evelyn-White, *Hesiod, the Homeric Hymns and Homerica* (London: W. Heinemann, 1914); from *Quintus Smyrnaeus* follow Alan James, *Quintus Smyrnaeus: The Trojan Epic (Posthomerica)* (Baltimore: Johns Hopkins University Press, 2004); from Herodotus follow George Rawlinson, *Herodotus. The Histories* (New York: Random House, 1997); and from the Hittite Ahhiyawa texts follow Gary Beckman, Trevor Bryce, and Eric H. Cline, *The Ahhiyawa Texts* (Atlanta: Society of Biblical Literature, 2011). Information regarding the finds from the recent excavations at Troy comes primarily from articles in the periodical *Studia Troica*, published annually from 1991 to 2009; many are in English but most are in German.

Chapter 2: The war in historical context

"The foreign countries made a conspiracy in their islands": Translation following W. F. Edgerton and J. A. Wilson, *Historical Records of Ramses III: The Texts in Medinet Habu*, vols. 1 and 2 (Chicago: University of Chicago Press, 1936), 53, pl. 46; revised translation found in J. A. Wilson, "The War Against the Peoples of the Sea," in *Ancient Near Eastern Texts Relating to the Old Testament, Third*

Edition with Supplement, ed. J. Pritchard, 262–63 (Princeton, NJ: Princeton University Press, 1969).

Chapter 3: Homeric questions

"invented by a single human being": Jay Tolson, "Was Homer a Solo Act or a Bevy of Bards? Classicists Have Few Clues but Lots of Theories," *US News and World Report*, July 24, 2000, 39; available online at: http://www.usnews.com/usnews/doubleissue/mysteries/ homer.htm (last accessed November 4, 2012).

Chapter 4: The Hittite texts

"As Tudhaliya the Great King shattered the Assuwa country": Translation following Ahmet Ünal, A. Ertekin, and I. Ediz, "The Hittite Sword from Bogazkoy—Hattusa, Found 1991, and Its Akkadian Inscription," *Muze* 4 (1991): 51.

"When They Came from Steep Wilusa": Calvert Watkins, "The Language of the Trojans," in *Troy and the Trojan War: A Symposium Held at Bryn Mawr College, October 1984*, ed. Machteld J. Mellink, 45–62, esp. pp. 58–62 (Bryn Mawr, PA: Bryn Mawr College, 1986).

"outright war, a skirmish or two, or merely a verbal dispute": Commentary by Trevor Bryce, in *The Ahhiyawa Texts*, ed. Gary Beckman, Trevor Bryce, and Eric H. Cline, 121 (Atlanta: Society of Biblical Literature, 2011).

Chapter 5: Early excavators

"cut out the Treasure with a large knife": David A. Traill, *Schliemann of Troy: Treasure and Deceit* (New York: St. Martin's Griffin, 1995), 111, quoting Heinrich Schliemann, *Troy and Its Remains: A Narrative of Researches and Discoveries Made on the Site of Ilium, and in the Trojan Plain* (New York: Benjamin Blom, Inc., 1875).

"The long dispute over the existence of Troy": Michael Wood, *In Search of the Trojan War*, 2nd ed. (Berkeley: University of California Press, 1996), 91, citing and translating Wilhelm Dörpfeld, *Troja und Ilion: Ergebnisse der Ausgrabungen in den vorhistorischen und historischen Schichten von Ilion, 1870–1894* (Athens: Beck & Barth, 1902).

"correspond with the observed facts": Carl W. Blegen, *Troy and the Trojans* (New York: Praeger, 1963), 145.

"even Dörpfeld had pointed out": Manfred Korfmann, "Die Arbeiten in Troia/Wilusa 2003; Work at Troia/Wilusa in 2003," *Studia Troica* 14 (2004): 5 and 14.

"we feel confident in attributing the disaster": Carl W. Blegen, John L. Caskey, and Marion Rawson, *Troy III: The Sixth Settlement* (Princeton, NJ: Princeton University Press, 1953), 331.

"the evidence supplied by the Cincinnati excavators": George Rapp Jr., "Earthquakes in the Troad," in *Troy: The Archaeological Geology*, ed. G. Rapp and J. A. Gifford, 55–56 (Princeton, NJ: Princeton University Press, 1982).

"everywhere marked by the ravages of fire": Carl W. Blegen, Cedric G. Boulter, John L. Caskey, and Marion Rawson, *Troy IV: Settlements VIIa, VIIb and VIII* (Princeton, NJ: Princeton University Press, 1958), 11–12.

"The fire-blackened wreckage": Carl W. Blegen, *Troy and the Trojans* (New York: Praeger, 1963), 162.

"an immediate reoccupation of the site": Carl W. Blegen, Cedric G. Boulter, John L. Caskey, and Marion Rawson, *Troy IV: Settlements VIIa, VIIb and VIII* (Princeton, NJ: Princeton University Press, 1958), 142.

"had we felt ourselves entirely free": Carl W. Blegen, Cedric G. Boulter, John L. Caskey, and Marion Rawson, *Troy IV: Settlements VIIa, VIIb and VIII* (Princeton, NJ: Princeton University Press, 1958), 144.

"excavated only with difficulty": Peter Jablonka, "Troy," in *The Oxford Handbook of the Bronze Age Aegean*, ed. Eric H. Cline, 853 (New York: Oxford University Press, 2010).

"a military event": Manfred Korfmann, "Troia—Ausgrabungen 1995," *Studia Troica* 6 (1996):7, see also 34–39.

"heaps of sling bullets": Manfred Korfmann, "Was There a Trojan War?" *Archaeology* 57/3 (2004): 37.

"due to destruction caused by war": Manfred Korfmann, "Die Arbeiten in Troia/Wilusa 2003; Work at Troia/Wilusa in 2003," *Studia Troica* 14 (2004): 15, table on 16.

"Now the evidence is burning and catastrophe with fire": Korfmann, in the transcript of the BBC documentary *The Truth of Troy*; http://www.bbc.co.uk/science/horizon/2004/troytrans.shtml (last accessed November 4, 2012).

"an unseemly bout of fisticuffs": Philip Howard, "Troy Ignites
    Modern-Day Passions," *Australian*, February 26, 2002, 12.

Epilogue

"the Trojan War motif": Susan Sherratt, "The Trojan War: History
    or Bricolage?" *Bulletin of the Institute for Classical Studies* 53.2
    (2010):5. See also similar statements by Kurt A. Raaflaub, "Homer,
    the Trojan War, and History," *Classical World* 91/5 (1998): 393.
"altered the details of actual historical events": Suzanne Saïd, *Homer
    and the Odyssey* (Oxford: Oxford University Press, 2011) 76–77.
"Was it so hard, Achilles, So very hard to die?": originally published
    in the *London Mercury* 1:3 (January 1920): 267; reprinted in
    Elizabeth Vandiver, *Stand in the Trench, Achilles: Classical
    Receptions in British Poetry of the Great War* (Oxford: Oxford
    University Press, 2010), 270–71.

Further reading

The Trojan War

Alexander, Caroline. *The War that Killed Achilles: The True Story of Homer's Iliad and the Trojan War*. New York: Viking, 2009.

Blegen, Carl W. *Troy and the Trojans*. New York: Praeger, 1963.

Bryce, Trevor L. "The Trojan War." In *The Oxford Handbook of the Bronze Age Aegean*, ed. Eric H. Cline, 475–82. New York: Oxford University Press, 2010.

Castleden, Rodney. *The Attack on Troy*. Barnsley, UK: Pen & Sword Books, 2006.

Dickinson, Oliver. "Was There Really a Trojan War?" In *Dioskouroi. Studies presented to W. G. Cavanagh and C. B. Mee on the anniversary of their 30-year joint contribution to Aegean Archaeology*, ed. C. Gallou, M. Georgiadis, and G. M. Muskett, 189–97. Oxford: Archaeopress, 2008.

Fields, Nic. *Troy c. 1700–1250 BC*. Oxford: Osprey Publishing, 2004.

Finley, Moses I. "The Trojan War." *Journal of Hellenic Studies* 84 (1964):1–9.

Graves, Robert. *The Siege and Fall of Troy*. London: The Folio Society, 2005.

Korfmann, Manfred. "Was There a Trojan War? Troy Between Fiction and Archaeological Evidence." In *Troy: From Homer's Iliad to Hollywood Epic*, ed. Martin M. Winkler, 20–26. Oxford: Blackwell, 2007.

Latacz, Joachim. *Troy and Homer: Towards a Solution of an Old Mystery*. New York: Oxford University Press, 2004.

Raaflaub, Kurt A. "Homer, the Trojan War, and History." *Classical World* 91/5 (1998): 386–403.

Sherratt, Susan. "The Trojan War: History or Bricolage?" *Bulletin of the Institute for Classical Studies* 53.2 (2010): 1–18.

Strauss, Barry. *The Trojan War: A New History.* New York: Simon & Schuster, 2006.

Thomas, Carol G., and Craig Conant. *The Trojan War.* Westport, CT: Greenwood Press, 2005.

Thompson, Diane P. *The Trojan War: Literature and Legends from the Bronze Age to the Present.* Jefferson, NC: McFarland, 2004. [Accompanying and updated website: http://novaonline.nvcc.edu/Eli/Troy/BbVersion/Troy/index.html]

Winkler, Martin M., ed. *Troy: From Homer's Iliad to Hollywood Epic.* Oxford: Blackwell, 2007.

Wood, Michael. *In Search of the Trojan War.* 2nd ed. Berkeley: University of California Press, 1996.

Homer and other early literary sources

Burgess, Jonathan S. *The Tradition of the Trojan War in Homer & the Epic Cycle.* Baltimore, MD: Johns Hopkins University Press, 2001.

Dalby, Andrew. *Rediscovering Homer: Inside the Origins of the Epic.* New York: W. W. Norton, 2006.

Finkelberg, Margalit, ed. *The Homer Encyclopedia.* 3 vols. Oxford: Wiley-Blackwell, 2011.

James, Alan. *Quintus Smyrnaeus: The Trojan Epic (Posthomerica).* Baltimore, MD: Johns Hopkins University Press, 2004.

Lord, Albert. With Steven Mitchell and Gregory Nagy, ed. *The Singer of Tales.* 2nd ed. Cambridge, MA: Harvard University Press, 2000.

Nagy, Gregory. *The Best of the Achaeans: Concepts of the Hero in Archaic Greek Poetry.* Baltimore, MD: Johns Hopkins University Press, 1979.

Parry, Adam, ed. *The Making of Homeric Verse: The Collected Papers of Milman Parry.* Oxford: Oxford University Press, 1971.

Powell, Barry B. *Homer.* 2nd ed. Oxford: Wiley-Blackwell, 2007.

Powell, Barry B. *Homer and the Origin of the Greek Alphabet.* Cambridge: Cambridge University Press, 1996.

Saïd, Suzanne. *Homer and the Odyssey.* Oxford: Oxford University Press, 2011.

Thomas, Carol G., ed. *Homer's History: Mycenaean or Dark Age?* Huntington, NY: Robert E. Krieger, 1977.

West, Martin L. "The Invention of Homer." *Classical Quarterly* 49 (1999): 364–82.

Willcock, Malcolm. "Neoanalysis." In *A New Companion to Homer*, ed. Ian Morris and Barry B. Powell, 174–92. Leiden: Brill, 1997.

Achilles and Helen of Troy

Austin, Norman. *Helen of Troy and Her Shameless Phantom*. Ithaca, NY: Cornell University Press, 2008.

Hughes, Bettany. *Helen of Troy: Goddess, Princess, Whore*. New York: Knopf, 2005.

Maguire, Laurie. *Helen of Troy: From Homer to Hollywood*. Oxford: Wiley-Backwell, 2009.

Shay, Jonathan. *Achilles in Vietnam: Combat Trauma and the Undoing of Character*. New York: Simon & Schuster, 1995.

Archaeology of Troy

Blegen, Carl W. *Troy and the Trojans*. New York: Praeger, 1963.

Blegen, Carl W., John L. Caskey, and Marion Rawson. *Troy III: The Sixth Settlement*. Princeton, NJ: Princeton University Press, 1953.

Blegen, Carl W., Cedric G. Boulter, John L. Caskey, and Marion Rawson. *Troy IV: Settlements VIIa, VIIb and VIII*. Princeton, NJ: Princeton University Press, 1958.

Dörpfeld, Wilhelm. *Troja und Ilion: Ergebnisse der Ausgrabungen in den vorhistorischen und historischen Schichten von Ilion, 1870–1894*. Athens: Beck & Barth, 1902.

Jablonka, Peter. "Troy." In *The Oxford Handbook of the Bronze Age Aegean*, ed. Eric H. Cline, 849–61. New York: Oxford University Press, 2010.

Mountjoy, Penelope A. "The Destruction of Troia VIh." *Studia Troica* 9 (1999): 253–93.

Mountjoy, Penelope A. "Troia VII Reconsidered." *Studia Troica* 9 (1999): 295–346.

Schliemann, Heinrich. *Ilios: the City and Country of the Trojans*. New York: Benjamin Blom, Inc., 1881.

Schliemann, Heinrich. *Troy and Its Remains: A Narrative of Researches and Discoveries Made on the Site of Ilium, and in the Trojan Plain*. New York: Benjamin Blom, 1875.

Heinrich Schliemann

Allen, Susan Heuck. *Finding the Walls of Troy: Frank Calvert and Heinrich Schliemann at Hisarlik*. Berkeley: University of California Press, 1999.

Boedeker, Deborah, ed. *The World of Troy: Homer, Schliemann, and the Treasures of Priam*. Proceedings from a Seminar sponsored by the Society for the Preservation of the Greek Heritage and held at the Smithsonian Institution on February 21–22, 1997. Washington, DC: Society for the Preservation of the Greek Heritage, 1997.

Calder, William A. III, and David A. Traill. *Myth, Scandal and History: The Heinrich Schliemann Controversy and a First Edition of the Mycenaean Diary*. Detroit, MI: Wayne State University Press, 1986.

Schuchhardt Carl. *Schliemann's Excavations: An Archaeological and Historical Study*; New York: Macmillan and Co., 1891.

Traill, David A. *Excavating Schliemann: Collected Papers on Schliemann*. Atlanta: Scholars Press, 1993.

Traill, David A. *Schliemann of Troy: Treasure and Deceit*. New York: St. Martin's Griffin, 1995.

Hittites

Bryce, Trevor. *The Kingdom of the Hittites*. New ed. New York: Oxford University Press, 2005.

Bryce, Trevor. *Life and Society in the Hittite World*. Oxford: Oxford University Press, 2004.

Bryce, Trevor. *The Trojans and Their Neighbors*. London: Routledge, 2006.

Bryce, Trevor. *The World of the Neo-Hittite Kingdoms: A Political and Military History*. New York: Oxford University Press, 2012.

Collins, Billie Jean. *The Hittites and Their World*. Atlanta: Society of Biblical Literature, 2007.

Mycenaeans

Castledon, Rodney. *The Mycenaeans*. London: Routledge, 2005.

Dickinson, Oliver T. P. K. *The Aegean Bronze Age*. Cambridge: Cambridge University Press, 1994.

Finley, Moses I. *The World of Odysseus*. New York: Penguin, 1956.

French, Elizabeth. *Mycenae: Agamemnon's Capital*. Oxford: Tempus, 2002.

Schofield, Louise. *The Mycenaeans*. Malibu, CA: J. Paul Getty Museum, 2007.

Sea Peoples

Cline, Eric H., and David O'Connor. "The Sea Peoples." In *Ramesses III: The Life and Times of Egypt's Last Hero*, ed. Eric H. Cline and David O'Connor, 180–208. Ann Arbor: University of Michigan Press, 2012.

Roberts, R. Gareth. *The Sea Peoples and Egypt*. PhD diss. Oxford: University of Oxford, 2008.

Sandars, Nancy. *The Sea Peoples: Warriors of the Ancient Mediterranean, 1250–1150 B.C.* 2nd ed. London: Thames and Hudson, 1985.

Index

Index

Index